Hard Faith

Hard Faith

A Final Memoir

Ray Lopez

Foreword by Paula Gill Lopez

RESOURCE *Publications* · Eugene, Oregon

HARD FAITH
A Final Memoir

Resource Publications
An Imprint of Wipf and Stock Publishers
199 W. 8th Ave., Suite 3
Eugene, OR 97401

www.wipfandstock.com

PAPERBACK ISBN: 978-1-5326-6404-5
HARDCOVER ISBN: 978-1-5326-6405-2
EBOOK ISBN: 978-1-5326-6406-9

.   NOVEMBER 24, 2021 9:15 AM

Unless otherwise noted, all scriptural references and quotes are taken from
the New International Version.

All royalties from the sale of Hard Faith will be donated to the ALS Association, MA Chapter.

I dedicate this book to my friend, Rich Macharolli, and my friend and sister-in-law, Mary Beth Lopez. They both fought ALS, this insidious disease, with faith, courage, and hope; and in doing so, taught me about the power of God's love.

Contents

Foreword

Paula Gill Lopez

Now faith is the substance of things hoped for,
the evidence of things not seen.

~HEBREWS 11:1 KJV

If *Hope is the thing with feathers,*[1] Faith is the thing with deep roots in firm fertile ground.

Faith ignites the Spirit like a colossal kaleidoscope on a fourth of July night.

Faith trusts that cold gray February days will unfurl in buds that herald spring.

There are faith testers and there are faith builders. In our life, we have experienced both. Some of which you will read about in this book.

Faith believes that seemingly impossible things are possible.

Faith is the glue that has held our marriage together for 40 years.

---

1. Dickinson, The Complete Poems of Emily Dickenson

Lately, when I think about the life Ray has lived, the events that have led him—us—to this moment, I think about Queen Esther and the words of her Uncle Mordecai.

"And who knows whether you have not come to the kingdom for such a time as this?" Esther 4:14 ESV

For such a time as this.

Looking back, it is much easier to see how the cliff-hugging, zigzagging, high and low, sometimes dead-end road got us here. God writes straight with crooked lines.

Ask the Dean who expelled Ray in high school if he thought Ray would end up where he is now; I suspect he would laugh in disbelief.

Ask the same of Mr. Spofford, beloved high school math teacher; he would smile knowingly. He had faith.

"for we live by faith, not by what we see with our eyes." ~

Ray's life experiences reveal a constant tension between light and darkness. While God always encourages potential; the devil is right there to tempt and seduce.

Racism throughout elementary, middle and high school;

descension into substance induced nightmares beginning at age eleven;

obsession with lifting weights like his life depended on it;

a short stint in jail as a precursor to spending his 19th birthday in a psychiatric hospital.

For such a time as this.

Being granted early release from probation to relocate;

escaping from NY to connect with his roots in southern California;

reimagining his Hispanic heritage as a source of pride rather than impediment;

graduating with his BA and then his MA in English at UC Berkeley facilitating his remarkable hire as a US Probation Officer.

For such a time as this.

But the devil does not give up, which is why we're instructed:

Be sober, be vigilant; because your adversary the devil walks about like a roaring lion, seeking whom he may devour. Resist him, steadfast in the faith ~1 Peter 5:8-9 NKJV

The devil has had designs on Ray his whole life. But God's protection has been ever-present. In this, Ray's third book, you can see God's hand clearly, more so than in his first or even second book. But just as God never gives up on us, the devil never stops trying to recruit us.

Be sober. Be vigilant. *Always.* For such a time as this.

I've borne witness to the after-midnight paralysis resulting from tormentors that have pursued Ray throughout his life. But they never followed him into the daylight.

Mandatory retirement at age 57 was much too soon;

losing his beloved dad suddenly before he was ready;

debilitated by grief - unable to get out of bed - to function;

thinking about ending the anguish unspeakably.

"Get out of bed," I finally told him angrily, impatiently. "I never thought you, of all people, would give up. YOU HAVE TO FIGHT."

I have given you authority to trample on snakes and scorpions and to overcome all the power of the enemy; nothing will harm you. ~ Luke 10:19 NIV

For such a time as this.

In his retirement, Ray started a private business as a federal sentencing consultant. The business divinely morphed into death penalty mitigation. Given his own background, Ray effortlessly builds a unique rapport with his clients, "connecting with the hardcore —one at a time," as was prophesied many years ago. "Evangelist, evangelist, evangelist." All the emotional discomfort, unkindness, and self-destruction facilitates relationships with men, some barely men, in prison who are eligible for the death penalty. They sense Ray understands and some part of him is like them.

For such a time as this.

Using Ray's life experiences and malleability, God created a man who, in the midst of worldly distractions, is devoted to Jesus. I say emphatically, Ray lives his faith out loud. LOUDLY out loud.

God uses all things for the good of those who are called according to His purpose. ~Romans 8:28

IF WE LET HIM.

For such a time as this.

God has led him here, getting paid by the government as a mitigation specialist. Meeting men in orange jumpsuits for sacred appointments. Sharing who he is and whose he is.

Ray's mantra these days and the primary mission of his life can be found in Romans 10:

If you declare with your mouth, "Jesus is Lord," and believe in your heart that God raised him from the dead, you will be saved. ~Romans 10:9

Everything Ray experienced—what's in and left out of his books— has laid a foundation for him to do his real work. In the five years since Ray retired, ten of his clients have given their life to Christ in prison.

Positioned by God. For such a time as this.

We love to listen to a song co-written and sung by Dolly Parton and Zach Williams. The words narrate Ray's life journey and that of many of us.

In the waiting, in the searching

In the healing and the hurting

Like a blessing buried in the broken pieces

Every minute, every moment

Where I've been and where I'm going

Even when I didn't know it or couldn't see it

There was Jesus

In the best of times, faith shouts, "Thank you, Jesus!"

In the worst of times, faith whimpers in stillness, knowing He is God.

In ALL times, faith must be active.

Hard [tough, challenging, undeniable, unbreakable, true] faith.

Acknowledgements

I GIVE THANKS TO MY LORD and Savior, Christ Jesus, for always guiding me through the odyssey of my life. I thank my amazingly wonderful wife, Paula, for loving me, believing in me, and teaching our children how to love unconditionally and laugh in the joy. I thank my daughter, Tebben, for sharing her artistic vision and her critical reading of my words. I thank my son, Jesse, for embracing my sports teams, occasionally playing me in chess, and helping me to laugh at myself. I thank my siblings, Teresa, Steve, and Pete for carefully reading the stories about our parents, the ups and downs, as Dad would say, and adding their own memories and stories that enhanced the narrative. This is also their story, and I am blessed by their support. A special thanks to Teresa for the beautiful sketches she drew of our parents and Mary and Steve. I thank my brother in Christ, John Wood, for allowing me to share his amazing testimony. I thank Brother Jerry for always reminding me that spiritual covenants are for life. I thank my copy editor, Rich Gelfand, for his careful reading and questions/suggestions on the text. Finally, I thank my publisher, Wipf and Stock, for believing in me and blessing me with the gift of patience.

Chapter 1

Princess Wenonah Drive

WE FINALLY BOARD AND settle in our seats in the front of the flight attendants' station, which provides extra legroom and space for Tebb to play at our feet. The plane takes off; I feel a part of me dying, and I cry. I've grown into manhood in California and left childish things behind. I married Paula, stopped drinking and drugging, was baptized in the Holy Spirit, found a church, found a career, earned a graduate degree, bought a home, and it was there we welcomed Tebben into the world. Halfway through the flight, Tebb is tired and cold. I ask a flight attendant for a blanket so she can take a nap on the floor of the bulkhead. I'm not surprised when I hear "There are no more blankets available." But I am surprised by the act of kindness shown by the oversized lady sitting across the aisle. She loans us a pair of her shorts which make a perfect blanket, and Tebb sleeps away until she is awoken by the pain in her ears popping to the pressure of our descent. It's been a long, hard journey back east, and I know I cannot go forward in my own strength. No.

But I also know I won't have to. I know "I can do all things through Christ who strengthens me." Philippians 4:13 (NKJV)

We arrive at my parents' house in Commack before our fleet of three vehicles shows up the next day, followed by our material lives packed into a tractor-trailer meeting us in Shelton the day after. The move to Shelton, Connecticut, requires all hands-on deck.

Shelton is a perfect distance, not too close and not too far. It's only thirty miles to Commack as the crow flies to 4 Sarina Drive. The Larkfield Pub, aka "The Twilight Zone," has been replaced by a dry cleaner. It's about 50 yards from my parents' house, which was some small grace in the darkness, as I could crawl home if necessary. And there are other changes.

Paula's sister, Carla, found a home for us to rent in the White Hills section of Shelton. White Hills still has small ranches, some cattle, old woods and 19th Century remnants scattered about. The house is on Princess Wenonah Drive. Princess Wenonah. Princess Wenonah. Princess Wenonah is fun to say. It sounds a little magical. Princess Tebben lives on Princess Wenonah Drive. The house is on top of a good-sized little hill. The paved driveway offers a 40% grade that rounds into the parking area in front of a two-car garage. It's a quiet neighborhood. We can hear our neighbor's conversations on still, silent nights. So, it's Paula, Tebben, me, and "Mama's Stupid Dissertation" living on Princess Wenonah Drive. I don't recall ever calling it Mama's Stupid Dissertation. Tebben takes the copyright on that one. She's such a perceptive little girl.

I do a little research and come to find that Wenonah is a Dakota Sioux character in a "Lover's Leap" romantic legend set at Maiden Rock, which is on the Wisconsin side of Lake Pepin. Rather than marry a suitor she does not love, Wenonah chooses to leap from the cliff off Maiden Rock to her death. There are three levels of rocks, from the edge of the small front yard down to the street. One missed step could result in a broken leg. Death is not likely. However, the driveway becomes my nemesis.

Paula gets right back to finishing her dissertation, and I have a month before starting work. There's a little swing set in the backyard, a small area backed by more rocks continuing up the hill. We place a small plastic pool near the swings, and Tebb, at three years old, is content to splash around.

God's grace is poured out in timely portions. I am originally told that my duty station would be the U.S. Probation Office in Hartford, a 100-mile round trip. But when Chief Judge Jose Cabranes finds out that Paula will be working in Fairfield and we are living in Shelton, he tells my chief, Maria Rodriguez McBride, to place me in the Bridgeport office, a 22-mile round trip. So instead of spending two hours a day commuting, I'm looking at a half-hour on a typical day. Fortunately, there's a pull-up bar in the house, and I get by with pushups, pull-ups and sit-ups every day. I'm about to turn 35 and although I've spent the last 14 years bulking up to a 225-lb bodybuilding physique, I still feel light on my feet and decide to mix it up a bit by running sprints up our steep driveway.

I'm feeling good doing the work until my right calf explodes halfway up the third sprint. It feels like I've been hit with a twelve-pound sledgehammer! I'm diagnosed with a torn plantaris tendon. I've never heard of it. The tendon is essentially useless in adults, unless you do a lot of crawling around like a baby. It's often used to repair a pitcher's shoulder during Tommy John surgery. It hurts like hell when you tear it and results in extreme swelling and bruising. Surgery isn't necessary. You just have to stay off your feet, elevate, and ice the calf. And so it goes. I'm immobilized for a couple of weeks and end up limping into work on the first day.

Our adjustment to living back east is difficult. Paula is working on her dissertation full-time. I'm lying on the couch with ice on my calf, and Tebb's an active three-year-old. After a couple of weeks, we decide that I should take Tebben with me to my parents so Paula can finish without any distractions. I'm still suffering from California separation anxiety. Paula and I haven't *really* talked since our flight, and I'm still angry. When we get to Commack, my mother and sister perceive that our marriage is under strain. Well, we are hitting some major marks on the stress-o-meter: a huge move, the start of Paula's academic career, a new world of federal probation for me and the changing tides of Tebben. The plan is for Paula to finish her dissertation before we return, or I have to start work. Ed and Hope, across the street from my parents, give us the tickets, Paula takes a break, and we go to a James Taylor Concert at Jones Beach on August 30, 1994. The drive out is a little strange and awkward because we know people are worried about our marriage, but *we* know we'll be okay. As others see it, life has dimmed the shine a bit; we're no longer "the perfect couple." We leave after the second song, "Oh I've seen fire and I've seen rain. I've seen lonely days that I thought would never end."

Chapter 2

Back to Work

WE BOTH START WORK on September 1, and Paula files her dissertation on October 20. I don't know much about Connecticut crime and punishment. I know that Bridgeport has a tough reputation. Otherwise, my impression of the state is based on the television show *Who's the Boss* with Tony Danza, Judith Light, and Alyssa Milano, and the movie *A Christmas in Connecticut* starring Barbara Stanwyck. In my mind, Connecticut is mostly rural, sleepy New England.

I heard there was some gang activity, but I'm feeling confident, like I can run a gang unit all by myself. After all, I'm coming from Oakland and the streets of San Francisco! Shortly after we moved to the Bay Area in '86, we watched live coverage of a massive funeral procession for a local drug dealer, Felix Mitchell, from East Oakland. There were thousands of people lining the streets. I learned that Felix Wayne Mitchell Jr. (August 23, 1954 – August 21, 1986) was a convicted drug lord and leader of the "69th Street Mob" criminal organization, which operated throughout California and into the Midwest. He was known as "Felix the Cat" after the cartoon character. He was seen as a Robin Hood figure within the community, like John Gotti. In addition to his calculated, cold-blooded, murderous ways, there are many stories of his courage and loving kindness. Like the story I hear in the early 90s from Timothy Bluitt, the lead defendant in a large racketeering indictment against the 69th Street Mob. He was the leader of the gang and my first assignment investigating the lead defendant in a multi-defendant case. When he was about six or seven years old, Felix Mitchell saved him from being wounded during a drive-by shooting by covering Bluitt's body with his own. Bluitt was Mitchell's eventual successor. Under his leadership, the gang expanded its territory, increased the armory to include machine guns and assault rifles, had an FBI clerk as an informant, and funded MC Hammer's first demo tape. I'm always amazed at the polarizing dichotomy one finds within criminal organizations like the Mafia and drug-trafficking gangs. I met Timothy's mother, a loving, nurturing Christian woman. He loves her dearly, yet when I listen to the taped conversation in which Bluitt threatens to murder a rival's entire family, I believe him. It's like being a psychopath with a dissociative disorder.

I have a lot to learn about organized crime in Connecticut. In 1993 there were 43 murders in Bridgeport, a city of 100,000, placing it as the murder capital of the country for cities with a population of 100,000. I'm knowledgeable about gangs and dealt mostly with the Black Gorilla Family (BGF), the Hells Angels, and the Aryan Brotherhood in the Bay Area.

I supervised a couple of guys who were members of the BGF, a prison gang that evolved from some Black Panthers incarcerated in California during the 70s. To become an elite member, you have to murder somebody and have "187" (the California Penal Code for murder) tattooed on your forehead. The BGF is based primarily in Oakland, and their main source of revenue is generated by extorting and robbing money from local drug dealers. How's that for tough?

I'm quickly blown away to learn that there are an estimated 7,000 card-carrying members (literally!) of the Latin Kings spread throughout the state with connections to New York. The cities of Bridgeport, New Haven, Meriden, and Hartford were organized with presidents, vice presidents, sergeants at arms, lieutenants, and soldiers. A personnel file was kept on each member. The Almighty Latin King and Queen Nation originated in Chicago in the 1950s, evolving from car clubs and neighborhood groups. A couple of federal inmates from Connecticut, Nelson Millet from Bridgeport, and Pedro Millan from Hartford, spent some prison time in Illinois and came back with the Charter and message. Early on there was a schism between them, and the Los Solidos was born under Millan's leadership. Violence between the two gangs was rampant, fueled by the crack cocaine market. The Latin Kings had a Crown Board of Directors, comprised of five members representing the five-pointed crown. There were regional commanders responsible for collecting taxes from each of these cities.

The Latin Kings are an equal opportunity organization, standing against sexual and racial/ethnic discrimination, while promoting education and community service. Their message to the public is that they represent a cultural movement to promote ethnic pride among Latinos. They are involved in food drives, holiday toy runs, and the Charter requires that members either have their high school diploma or are working toward obtaining it.

Beatrice Codiani, a woman of *Italian* ancestry (that's Latin enough), was a member of the Crown Board, which also included Doctor Eduardo Baez, a psychologist, who was the head of the New Haven School District Psychology Department. He went into private practice, opened three offices, and conducted forensic psych evaluations for the state courts. This is how he met the Latin Kings and started going to their meetings "to get to know them better." Maria Vidro was the president of the New Haven Chapter and was convicted of ordering a triple homicide, carried out by her husband, Johnny Zapata. You can see who wore the pants in that family and consider the things we do for love.

In the early 90s the U.S. Attorney's Office in Connecticut was the first in the United States to use the federal racketeering statutes to prosecute drug trafficking organizations. The Latin Kings provided adequate evidence in addition to wiretaps, informants, undercover work, and surveillance provided by the government. Beyond the personnel files and ID cards, the Charter itself made indirect but obvious instructions for carrying out murder. At that time two words could kill; all one needed was the "green light."

Common sayings like "Don't make a federal case out of it," are firmly grounded in the reality that the feds take the big cases. Consequently, federal probation officers have the opportunity to investigate and supervise famous and infamous people. Leona Helmsley is being paroled after serving time at the Federal Correctional Institution at Danbury, Connecticut, for tax fraud. She is the owner of the Helmsley Real Estate Empire in Manhattan, along with her husband, Harry Helmsley. She could be considered a contemporary Marie Antoinette and is referred to as "The Queen of Mean" because of the tyrannical way she treated her employees and her attitude toward those less fortunate than herself, whom she referred to as "the little people." My supervisor, Ellis Gamble, decides to assign her case to an experienced officer, who wouldn't become distracted by her celebrity, someone who will treat her like everyone else under supervision—me.

I call Leona to introduce myself as her new probation officer and schedule our first office meeting. When I tell her she needs to come into the office she says, "Oh Mr. Lopez, I couldn't possibly do that." When I ask her why she explains, "I couldn't possibly leave Harry." Now Harry Helmsley is a real estate billionaire whose company is one of the country's biggest property holders, owning the Empire State Building and many of New York's most prestigious hotels. I know that Harry suffered a massive stroke and is non-ambulatory. I am looking forward to doing a home visit at the estate in Greenwich anyway, so I tell her it's fine and schedule the visit for the next day at 8:30 in the morning.

I'm driving our red 1985 Honda CRX south on the Merritt Parkway and get off at Round Hill Road in Greenwich, one of the wealthiest communities in the country. I'm driving through this deeply wooded area with million-dollar mansions abounding, when I see one that rises above the rest. It has a name; Dunnellen Hall sits atop a hill at 521 Round Hill Road. This 22,000-sq-ft mansion is situated on 40 acres enclosed with a spiked, ornate black iron fence. "Forget about it." I pull up to the front gate and marvel at the cobblestone road that winds up the hill to the residence. It is lined with antique lampposts. I press the intercom button. "Hello.

Can I help you?" "Yes. This is Ray Lopez, Mrs. Helmsley's probation officer here for my 8:30 appointment." Just a minute sir; someone will be there to meet you in a moment." I then see two men in
a golf cart coming down the road. The passenger is a well-dressed,
older white gentleman with short white hair, neatly trimmed with
a perfect part, and wearing a gray suit, white shirt, and red tie. The
driver is a young Latino lad, in his early twenties, wearing blue
jeans, a white tee shirt, and a red paisley bandana around his neck.
"Mr. Irish Name" identifies himself as the head of Helmsley security and a retired NYPD homicide detective. He doesn't ask to see
my identification, which makes me think they've already checked
me out. I follow the cart about a quarter mile up the cobblestone
road until we drive up to an oval fountain, about half the length of
a football field, and park.

I am led into the estate through the kitchen. This is my first
clue. I've never been in the kitchen of a five-star restaurant, but
I imagine this is what it looks like. It must be at least 1000 sq ft,
stainless steel glistening everywhere. The kitchen is to my left. On
the right I see a caged vault, like you'd see in a large bank. It's open
and there are classical candelabras being polished by a housemaid.
I guess it's the day they polish the silver. I am led into a large foyer
area that connects with the dining room and an Olympic-sized
indoor pool. The long dining room has a large table with 20 or
more chairs, and the whole thing is done in French Colonial; at
least I think it's French Colonial; but what do I know?

Leona Helmsley floats across the room and enters the foyer.
She is quite petite, with shortly cropped brown hair, high cheek-
bones, and wearing lots of makeup. I don't remember what clothes
she wore but she has Kelly Green eyes that do not blink. I've never
seen such deep green eyes and wonder if she's wearing contacts.
She greets me with "Hello Mr. Lopez. It's a pleasure to meet you."
She grabs my right hand, and we begin to shake hands. I am holding my briefcase containing my field book in my left hand. And
we shake without ceasing, while she stares into my eyes without
blinking and continues with "Mr. Lopez, we'll be meeting in the
Florida room to the left, if that's alright with you." And I look

and see the entrance to an indoor Olympic-size pool area, with salmon-colored tiled patios surrounding the pool. I look back and realize that she's still holding my hand, although the shaking has subsided somewhat. I slip my hand free, tell her the Florida room will be fine, and as we're about to enter she suddenly stops and asks "Mr. Lopez, would you like to leave your briefcase on this bench in the foyer? You don't have any money in it, do you?" This is surreal. I'm thinking out loud at this point and say, "Nope. I have twenty dollars in my pocket though. I'm a $20-a-week man, enough to keep me wired on coffee." To which she chuckles, "Ha ha ha." I've never put my briefcase down during a home visit before, but I do on this occasion, after extracting my notebook, a monthly report form, financial statement, and standard conditions of supervision. I don't know why. I figure I can see it from the room we'll be sitting in. I guess Leona's strange presence has me off kilter a bit.

We sit down on some plush, cushioned patio furniture, and I start the meeting by handing Leona the written monthly report she is required to complete. While I'm explaining how she must submit it within the first week of each month for the preceding month, she's on the telephone with one of her staff. She hangs up, and within seconds a very polished young woman with a British accent enters the room and quickly scurries away with instructions from Leona to complete the form. A section of the form requires a brief financial statement which is obviously inadequate for Leona's purposes, so I hand her the full financial statement. It is several pages long, and I tell her to have her accountant complete it for her and to sign and submit one each month. I get no complaints. I go over the conditions of supervision with her without much ado. Then she starts talking.

Leona launches into a pity party and starts lamenting about how unfairly she was treated by the IRS, the U.S. Attorney's Office, and even her own lawyer, Alan Dershowitz. She explains how she and her husband paid $150,000,000 in taxes for the years in question and paid back the $75,000,000 they allegedly owed and how the Government went out of its way in prosecuting and punishing her for their own personal reputations and rewards. I decided to let her talk and wait until the storm subsides, which it does after a few *very* long minutes. Then she says she wants me to meet Harry and places another call. After a few moments, Mr. Helmsley appears in the foyer with a private nurse pushing his wheelchair. He is wheeled onto the patio, and I can see that not only is he non-ambulatory, but he's also a quadriplegic and has lost the ability to speak. He is placed right next to my chair. Leona gets up, stands over her husband and says, "Harry dear, I want you to meet Mr. Lopez." She then lifts his right hand and pulls it a bit toward me. I reach over and shake his limp hand with Leona's left hand holding his wrist and her right hand covering our grip. This fortunately lasts only a couple of seconds in comparison to Leona's handshake, but I'm still feeling like I'm in an episode of *Night Gallery*. Harry is wheeled away and I'm ready to leave. During our preliminary departure small talk, Leona turns to me and says, "Oh Mr. Lopez, before you leave, I want you to know that I'm having a barbeque for the help this weekend and you and your wife and children are welcome to come." I think, *Oh my God! You've got to be kidding me! What people say about you is true. You are the Queen of Mean. I'm your probation officer not one of the help. You need to answer to me.* Instead, I reply, "No thank you Mrs. Helmsley, but thank you for the invitation." And now we're standing in the foyer again. I have my briefcase and I'm ready to leave. Leona has captured my hand again and is shaking it vigorously for far too long and staring into my eyes with her dark, unblinking green eyes when she says, "Mr. Lopez, you can't imagine what's it's like being me." And as I free my hand from her grip, I agree that "No. I certainly cannot." Then I turn and leave through the kitchen.

Leona reaffirms what scripture has taught me about the love of money: it is the source of all sorts of evil and makes narrow the gate to heaven. And I learn from Leona that the price she is paying is *loneliness*.

Thereafter, she calls me every day, not to ask for anything or with any questions but just to talk. This goes on for months, and I come to know that Leona Helmsley, the richest person I've ever met and one of the richest people in the world, must also be one of the saddest, loneliest people, a prisoner in her own home, her heart, and in her mind.

After six months Judge Cabranes gets appointed to the 2nd Circuit Court of Appeals, and my chief places me in the New Haven office because they "need a presentence report writer there." Downtown New Haven is 21 miles from our house, twice as far as Bridgeport. Presentence investigators are assigned cases all over the state. It doesn't really matter what office is your duty station. The Hartford Office is in the federal courthouse on Main Street. The Bridgeport office is in the federal courthouse on Lafayette Boulevard and the New Haven office is in the financial center on the historic green, right next to the historic federal courthouse. Downtown New Haven is great. Yale University is in the center of it all, and there are there are about 100 restaurants to choose from.

When I get to New Haven, I realize the office tone is dramatically different than Bridgeport. There's a silent battle line drawn between the officers and support staff. At this point in my career, I'm probably the only officer in the country who still dictates reports. Officers are writing and editing their reports in WordPerfect. I love dictation. Not everyone can do it. It's a different writing process. Baby Boomers have learned to write through a visual and tactile process, pencil to paper. Dictation is all cerebral and fast. I'm at the point where I can see an entire paragraph in my mind. The clerks hate it.

I've never taken shit from anyone. I've always treated people with respect and consideration, and I expect the same in return. During the time I'm in New Haven, I have more than a few conversations with clerks concerning our working relationship. By the time I transfer back to Bridgeport five years later, the chief clerk identifies me as their number one problem. And so it goes.

The dynamic thing about the federal system is that you deal with everyone, from a 19-year-old kid selling crack on a street corner to a state governor accepting bribes and gratuities. There are people who are just angry they got caught, like a lot of high-level, white-collar fraudsters who look to blame others, don't accept responsibility, and plead guilty because it's the best deal they can make. They can be addicted to power and money. Then there are honest criminals—like mob guys and gang-bangers—who don't pretend to be anything but what they are, criminals. They don't make excuses. It's the cost of doing business. We speak the truth to each other and sometimes their truth is to abscond, because they know they're screwing up and you're going to get a warrant for their arrest. But everyone has a different truth, a lesson shared by one of the guys I investigated.

Jimmy was a mobbed-up, trash-hauling tyrant in Fairfield County. He had his own fleet of trucks and roll-offs, but his main influence came through the transfer stations he owned. Everyone knew he paid tribute to one of the New York "Families" and that you had to "pay to play" if you wanted to pick up and dump. He told you how much to bid on a job and would let you have your little slice of the pie. Jimmy pled out to a racketeering conspiracy and entered into a fairly comprehensive plea agreement in which he agreed to forfeit $10,000,000 in assets and serve between seven and nine years in prison. Jimmy was living the life. He had a new wing of the local hospital named in his honor after he paid for the elaborate expansion. He also had *la mantenuta*, his mistress, nicely set up with a ranch and horses. She also answered the phones at the shop.

We're doing the initial interview in my office in Bridgeport; Jimmy's attorney, Huey, is a very well-known, well-established lawyer in Connecticut. He's with Jimmy; in the federal system, attorneys are almost always at presentence interviews because anything a defendant says to the probation officer can have a direct impact on their sentence. I'm asking questions about his personal history, specifically marital history. I ask my basic questions about the nature of the marriage and any history of serious marital problems, as I do in every case. But before I allow Jimmy to answer, as usual, I define what I mean by serious marital problems to include any forms of domestic abuse, substance abuse, infidelities, and financial problems. He knows that I know about at least two affairs, both women having been indicted in the case. He looks at Huey who, even though he knows better, is still representing his client and asks me the need for such questioning. So I go into my tutorial speech about how examining one's relationships is the best way I know of assessing that person's character, which is imperative, and statutorily required, in determining a fair sentence. And a spouse is usually the most important relationship to understand. He tells me he has had affairs. When I ask how many, he answers, "I don't know, two or three." I move on. At the end of the interview, I schedule a home visit with Jimmy. As I am escorting them out of the office, Huey asks me to not get into this marital discussion with Jimmy's wife during the home visit. I tell them not to worry, that I only plan to ask her the same questions I asked Jimmy, without volunteering anything I know or leading her in any way. If she wants to talk about the marriage so be it. If not, that's fine as well. She's not convicted or awaiting sentencing, but everyone in the family is being sentenced in their own way.

During the home visit I'm meeting with Roseanne, Jimmy's wife, in the spacious kitchen of their 10,000-sq-ft home. We're talking privately, which is my preference in collateral interviews. When I get to marital history and ask her the same questions about any history of serious marital problems, she tells me about his affairs. Now attorneys don't usually attend home visits, but as you can see, Jimmy is a special guy. Huey doesn't come, but his very attractive young assistant, blond-haired, blue-eyed Tabitha, is in attendance and talking with Jimmy in another room while Roseanne and I talk in the kitchen. As we exit, getting ready for my tour of the home, I see Tabitha on the phone in a sitting room near the front door. She has a sheepish look on her face and tells me that Huey's on the phone and wants to talk to me. "What?!" I say incredulously, and Tabitha nods her head in affirmation trying not to make eye contact. I take the phone and hear Huey say, "Ray! What the fuck? You said you weren't going to talk to her about the affairs!" Click. I hang up the phone. I figure they must've had the kitchen wired. I take the tour and am very impressed by the home gym. Before I depart, Jimmy and I have a final chat in front of the house." He says to me, "You know, Ray, there are usually three truths. For example, there's my truth, the government's truth, and the real truth which can be found somewhere in between." And that is true in most cases of defining truth between two parties. Profound, really.

Meanwhile at Fairfield University, Paula is the program director and single faculty member of the School Psychology Program, which is part of the Graduate School of Education and Allied Professions (GSEAP). Fairfield University is a private Jesuit school in Fairfield, Connecticut. It was founded by the Society of Jesus in 1942 and is one of 28 member institutions of the Association of Jesuit Colleges and Universities. Fairfield is an affluent community just south of Bridgeport, which like other communities in Connecticut, provides stark contrast in socio-economic class. The campus is lovely and sits on top of a hill with views of the Long Island Sound. There are approximately 5,000 students, including the students of the GSEAP, the only graduate school at the time. Paula remains a one-person program for the next 11 years.

And her growing stress is compounded by the fact that we are in a traditional marriage. She cooks, is the primary parent, and does the laundry. I mow the lawn, barbeque, make breakfast, change light bulbs, and do the heavy lifting. A lot of the time, I also load and empty the dishwasher. And, I play with the kids! We've always been in a traditional marriage, but I'm not sure how exactly this happened. My parents both had full-time careers. My mom was a registered nurse, and my dad was an electronic engineer. I guess the imprint came from Paula's family. Her parents were huge underachievers. They met at Columbia, where my mother-in-law, Gloria, was the only female student in the Chemistry Department. She was also a Vogue model. My father-in-law, Bill, earned his degree in Psychology. Gloria never finished and became a home-maker. Bill went into banking but got lost in the two-hour martini lunches. Or perhaps it was the result of the Post-World War II, Golden Era, Jungian Collective Unconscious.

Regardless, our circumstances eventually caused Paula to go into early menopause, and things didn't improve until she righteously demanded help, primarily in the form of doing laundry. I was blind but now I see, and I see my laundry indefinitely piled into overflowing bins. I end up living out of one laundry basket, recycling the same clothes. I leave my other clothes behind, like the childish things I've left behind, and the active sinning. But the remnants remain, a reminder of the clothes I used to wear. This is not exactly Paula's vision, but she's no longer doing our laundry, which is good, and there's plenty of room for my improvement.

One of the great blessings in our lives is Paula's tenure track position at Fairfield, which provides the opportunity for our kids to attend one of the 27 colleges and universities within the Jesuit/ Catholic consortium with free tuition. The consortium includes schools such as Boston College, Creighton, Georgetown, Gonzaga, Loyola, and many other fine institutions. Trusting that our children will get accepted to Fairfield or one of these other schools, we decide, in faith, that there's no need for us to save money for their education. We purchase our home in Shelton in March 1995. Including a finished basement, the colonial has four bedrooms, two-and-a-half baths and is approximately 2500 square feet. It's on a shy two-acre lot with Daffodil Pond in the backyard. The pond is about a quarter of an acre and is fed by an underground spring, which overflows into the wetlands behind the pond during the rainy season. We've got woods on both sides of the house and share a wild kingdom with the deer, the Great Blue Heron, the Great White Egret, the tri-colored Egret, Red-Tailed Hawks, turkey vultures, muskrats, snapping turtles, catfish, water snakes, wild turkeys, and bats. There are also bobcats and coyotes to watch out for. The pond is also surrounded by woods, which creates a natural amphitheater. We love watching God waving to us with wind blowing through the leaves on the top of the trees and serenading us with the peepers in the warm months.

My sister-in-law, Carla, moves in with us. She's working for AmeriCorps in Norwalk at the armory, which is set up as a soup kitchen. "Car" is 12 years younger than Paula. She used to come to my parents' house with Paula to go swimming in the pool, and I was the shallow end monster. I would grab her and catapult her high into the deep end. She was a good swimmer and loved it! Car is beautiful and very intelligent, a Smith graduate. She's 24, tall, with long auburn hair. She has freckles and looks like a model. She helps out with Tebb, who at this point is the only grandchild on the Gill side of the family. Sometimes she picks Tebb up at Teddy Bear Corner, a daycare in Fairfield, not far from the university. She and Tebb are close and share special times together. Like the day they're driving home from daycare. A driver cuts Car off in a rotary onto Black Rock Turnpike. Car reacts by spilling forth practically every curse word known to man preceded by "stupid" after which Tebb says to her, "Aunt Carla, don't say stupid."

We clear the woods on the left side of the pond and put in a fiberglass in-ground pool. Our plan is for the house to be a magnet for our children's friends. And it works out that way, for a small moment.

Chapter 3

Powerlifting

I'VE BEEN LIFTING IN gyms since I was eighteen, and I have to find
a place to train that's close to the Bridgeport office. At that time,
our administration was allowing three hours a week, paid time,
for exercise. A few years later we lost the time because someone
in the Bureau of Prisons complained that they weren't allotted the
same opportunity. I start training at a Gold's Gym in Black Rock.
It's a five-minute drive from the office and I lift during lunchtime,
usually an hour and a half a day, and flex my schedule to make sure
I have enough hours. That's usually not a problem because being a
federal probation officer is not a 40-hour-a-week job.

Black Rock is an upper-income area of Bridgeport that tries
very hard to disassociate from the city. It is near the Long Island
Sound and has some nice restaurants and beachfront areas. This is
not the Gold's where Arnold and Franco first trained. It is a clean
commercial gym where they don't allow chalk and don't want you
to make too much noise. The members are corporate types and the
annual membership fee is six hundred dollars! I've been deadlifting over 600 lbs. since I was 30. I'm now 35 and getting stronger.
I sneak chalk into the gym when I pull and make sure to clean
up the evidence after I'm done. I'm trying to bring my squat and
deadlift up to par. Lifting weights has been an essential part of my
daily therapeutic healing since I was 11. I was the skinny kid on the
block getting my ass kicked every day and finding my dad's old set

of York barbells in the basement was a spiritual goldmine. The very first time I strained with a heavy weight I made a loud noise. Call it grunting; call it groaning; call it screaming; I call it breathing. One day I'm doing vertical leg presses in the corner of the gym. I've got it stacked with about 450 lbs. in 45-lb. plates, and I'm pushing hard and breathing loud. When I finish my last set, I roll out from under the press and find a young woman in a staff T-shirt saying something to me. I can't really see her that clearly or hear what she's saying because I'm in "the white zone." It's the primal place one goes when doing maximum effort sets, when the blood pressure is highest and your pulse is still racing. I come back to the world and hear her introduce herself as the assistant manager and say, "You can't do that here." "Do what?" I ask. "That loud noise. You can't make that loud noise." "I'm just breathing." I say, "I'm not doing it intentionally. It's natural and just comes out of me when I lift heavy." She responds with, "Well you intimidate the women in the club." "What women?" I ask. "Has anyone complained? Do you have a petition signed against me?" She then declares that "Yes, many women have complained, and you just can't make that noise in the gym." I tell her that I don't believe that I'm violating any of the gym rules in the contract that I signed, and I want her to show me the contract and point out which rule I am violating.

I finish my workout, shower up and head for the front desk where my new friend is standing alongside another female staff member. She's trying to not make eye contact with me and probably hoping I just leave. I approach her and calmly ask to see the gym membership contract. She hands me one and advises that she has highlighted the rule I am violating. The rule she highlights says something to the effect that you can't abuse the equipment, and there's no shouting and using profanity. I tell her I don't think I'm violating that rule, that I don't abuse the equipment and I don't shout or use profanity, which requires the use of language. Again, I'm just breathing. I see that she's not really listening to me, so I decide to demonstrate the distinction by saying, "You see, I'm now getting louder, raising my voice, again using my words, and building up to a level where you could say that I am shouting, and I could add in some profanity for a fuller example of a violation of this rule!" I only have two weeks left on my membership, and I decide that I must find a new place to train. I bid her adieu for the last time.

I'm in the office all day and before I leave, I look in The Yellow Pages to locate the nearest gyms. I find South Side Gym on Stratford Avenue in Stratford on the Bridgeport border. I call and speak to the owner, Joe Sylvia. I quickly share my Gold's Gym story and he tells me that South Side is a hardcore powerlifting gym; I can use all the chalk and make all the noise I want, and he charges $240 a year. It's only a few miles from the courthouse. I drive there after work to check it out. I pull into the small parking lot and get out of my car. I'm still in my shirt and tie. There're three Harleys parked out front and a few guys hanging out. One of them, the owner, Joe Sylvia, has shoulder length hair and is smoking a cigar. The place is a dungeon of masochistic pleasure. I think it was an old auto shop. It's dirty and dusty. There are hundreds of pounds of 45s, lifting chains, dumbbells up to 150 lbs., two lifting platforms, two power racks, including a Monolift (which I would learn is a hydraulic squat rack used in competitive powerlifting), a couple of benches, and a cable crossover machine. I'm impressed but am ultimately dissuaded because there are no showers, just a small bathroom which is desperately in need of a good cleaning.

The next day I go to the Stratford Athletic Club, a few blocks away from South Side. I meet the manager, Steve Lewis, a well-muscled bodybuilder, standing about 6'4" and weighing around 250. I tell him the story about how, for all intents and purposes, I was kicked out of Gold's for being too loud. Like Joe, Steve tells me that I can make all the noise I want and use chalk, as long as I clean up after myself. As a bonus, he adds that there are some nationally ranked powerlifters that train there and have their own section of the gym. This is a surprise, as the Stratford club is really a racquetball club and family gym with an indoor track and pool. Not the kind of place where you would expect to see hardcore lifters. I am vaguely aware of powerlifting, having read some articles in *Iron Magazine*. And I remember seeing a couple of powerlifters train back when I was 18 or 19 before we moved to California. They were doing heavy box squats, something I didn't understand at the time. I'd also thought about competing in the deadlift in the Police Olympics, but I was just there to train and get stronger.

Absolute power is contagious, addictive, and powerlifters are like a family, a relatively small and often strange subculture of the lifting world. You need a lot of training partners to get strong and prepare for a competition because you need plenty of spotters for safety and the group energy and support to push beyond your limits to reach new goals. Powerlifters are attracted to others who are strong and look to recruit people into the sport. That's how I meet Andy Murray. He approaches me one day and starts telling me about their team, Flynn's Gym. Their leader, Tommy Flynn, is a retired Bridgeport cop who everybody calls Big Daddy. Their best lifter is Johnny Antignani, an excellent athlete who is an accomplished Olympic lifter and powerlifter. I consider Olympic lifting to be a real sport and something familiar to the general public. I loved watching Olympic lifting on TV and remember seeing the super-heavyweight Russian lifter, Alexia, breaking all those world records. The clean and press and the snatch are explosive moves that require agility and athleticism. Powerlifting is comprised of the three basic lifts: the squat, bench press, and deadlift. Technique and form are important, but speed and power are the essence. I join the team and Johnny A. writes up my first training cycle to compete in my first meet. As I start training with the team, consisting of 12 guys and one woman, I learn about gear. The sport offers divisions that allow supportive gear, bench shirts, and squat suits that add pounds to your lift. The gear is made of either denim or thick nylon material, which creates a super spring-like action off the bottom of the lift. You need assistance to get into your shirt or suit, and you can barely move once you're in. In a bench shirt you walk around like the Frankenstein monster. You need to learn how to use the equipment, which alters the natural leverages of your body, and you must put a heavy weight on the bar to even lower it to your chest, or squat below parallel. The material is so thick, and tightly fitted, that you can barely bend your elbows or knees unless a ponderous weight is added to gravity. Eventually, I get into a shirt that adds fifty pounds to my bench. In addition to the squat suit, you wrap your knees with thick nylon material with metal fibers. The combination of a squat suit, knee wraps, and a thick lifting belt can add over a hundred pounds to your squat.

My first meet is the Tri-State (CT, NY, NJ) American Power-lifting Association Championships in February 1996 at the Iron Island Gym in Oceanside, New York, which is on the South Shore of Long Island. I learn that the Iron Island Powerlifting Team is big time, and their gym is sort of a mecca of powerlifting on the East Coast. Their coach, and co-owner of the gym, Ken Leistner, has been around the sport since the beginning and is a well-known authority on training and recovery. The meet is crazy. One of the Iron Island lifters is smacking himself on the forehead with a 2x4 to psych himself up for his attempts and has a trickle of blood running down his face throughout the day. It's an all- day event, with about eighty lifters in multiple weight classes, similar to boxing divisions. Each lifter is allowed three attempts in each event, starting with the squat, then bench press, and ending with the deadlift. It's a family affair with parents, spouses, children, and girlfriends in attendance to cheer for their loved ones. My parents are there, along with Paula and Tebben. The highlight of the meet is seeing the great (at least in the powerlifting world) Pat Susco squat 900 lbs. in his bare feet in the 242-lb division (the lifter weighs between 220.4 and 242)! I end up squatting 500 lbs., benching 340, and deadlifting a disappointing 585 lbs. for a 1425-lb. total, which qualifies me for the AAU Lifetime Drug-Free Nationals to be held at Southern Connecticut State University in New Haven in a couple of months. It's a good start, and powerlifting becomes an essential part of my life.

Chapter 4

Jesse Boy

I KNOW PAULA FEELS guilt and pain over the time she is away from Tebb. But when they are together there is nothing else. They sleep together. They lock into one another every night before falling up into dreams, some remembered, others gone like a vapor. Tebb's hands are like a soft vice of focused love. They lay down facing each other; Tebb places her hands on Paula's cheeks and draws her in until their faces are pressed together, and they look deep into each other's eyes. And they fall asleep like that. The portrait is forever imprinted in my mind.

The Looking Glass

Thou art thy mother's glass, and she in thee
calls back the lovely April of her prime;[1]
Which is now, before, and yet to come:
Before, when she carried you in her womb
and loved you so . . .
before holding you in her arms.
Now that you are no longer a little baby
but a big girl who knows her mama's eyes
are green like the Ninja Turtles.
Now that you can see your reflection

1. Shakespeare, Sonnet 3

in her eyes
and her soul reaching through.
And as you and your mama grow up together
and figure out what you want to be,
you will always be together.
And I will live with this love
and watch
the looking glass
that binds you.
I remember when I first saw
the beauty in your mama's eyes,
the beauty
I now see in yours.

There will be more poems to write. Paula is pregnant again, and this time we're having a boy! Tebben wants to name him Felix, but after Paula tells her that people will call him Fe Fe, she agrees that Jesse is a better name. It means "*the Lord exists*" in Hebrew. Paula's pregnancy during her second year of teaching at Fairfield, while trying to build up her program and manage her home life, is still a blur of migraines, hot flashes, grading papers, and joy.

Jesse enters the world at Bridgeport Hospital on August 18, 1996. My mother-in-law, Gloria, is staying with us to watch Tebben. I'm in the delivery room trying to encourage Paula while she's in labor. I'm by her side holding her hand, and with each push I say "atta' way babe!" quite enthusiastically until she turns to me and with razor sharp focus says, "Do not say atta' way again." I watch him come through the vaginal portal. I'm like a catcher crouched low waiting for the pitch.

We bring him home after a couple of days and are literally walking toward the front door with Jesse as Tebben is coming out to wait for the bus to her first day of kindergarten! She's growing up and no longer needs to sleep with her mama. At four months old, he develops respiratory syncytial virus (RSV), a common, and very contagious, virus that infects the respiratory tract. For the next several months, we must use a nebulizer every night for 20 minutes to give Jesse liquid albuterol that will help his lungs grow. I cradle him each night at the kitchen table and hold the plastic mask over his face. God's grace is found in this machinery as the loud gurgling noise and strong vibration of the motor sings Jess to sleep each time. And Paula's love for our expanding family is heaven on earth.

Motherhood

She leans back in a nest of pillows,
her back firmly braced
at just the right incline,
her breasts hard and full
with the sweet milk
awaiting in concert
with the first awakening cry
calling from the mouth of her baby boy,
already sturdy, solid and strong,
a testament
of the purity of his mother's milk
and her love.
They are one.
He is locked on and sucking away
drinking
                deeply back
to innocent sleep.
They are joined by the five-year-old
daughtersister extraordinaire,
taking a short detour on a return trip from the potty.
She is drawn to the nest
like a fairy princess
sleepwalking in the heart of the night,
searching for a good scratching of the back.
Her artistry expands
to a wizardry of soft
motion of suckling
and scratching away time,
until time falls away
to the fullness of dawn.

As the great Yogi Berra said, "It's déjà vu all over again." Paula led us to Judson Memorial Baptist Church in Richmond, California, when Tebb was a toddler and we now find ourselves at Long Hill Baptist Church in Trumbull, Connecticut. Pastor Mark is a good ol' boy Southern Baptist preacher from North Carolina. His wife, Nancy, is a traditional Southern Baptist preacher's wife, totally devoted to God, her husband, her three children and the various women's ministries such as children's church. I spend the first six months waiting in the car with Jesse, while he snoozes, or driving around during the service so he'll fall asleep. The church is mostly White, representative of the community, with a few Black and Hispanic families and active ministries at the Bridgeport Rescue Mission, and Isaiah House, a halfway house in Bridgeport. We join the church family and get involved. There's a strong emphasis on the Gospel and evangelism, right in my wheelhouse. Pastor Mark gives an invitation to accept Christ at almost every sermon. And there's a powerful music ministry going on. Paula and I do special music, solos and duets, and join the choir that puts on a full Broadway-style Christmas musical every year.

There's also a men's gospel quartet at Long Hill, which I am asked to join after the tenor and his family leave the state. We pray and practice hard and God uses Kingdom Bound in a powerful way. We end up with a powerful ministry that takes us all over New England. We sing at churches, men's conferences, and end up cutting a CD down in North Carolina. Kingdom Bound becomes the anchor that keeps us at Long Hill much longer than God had planned.

From left to right: Fred Preston, Me, Rick Anderson, and Allen Seymour

Chapter 5

As

In 1984 Congress enacted the Sentencing Reform Act (SRA) to bring honesty to federal sentencing and reduce disparity around the county. The honesty component eliminated parole. A guy could be sentenced to twenty years for armed bank robbery but get paroled after ten and serve the rest of his sentence in the community. If he violated parole, he would lose his street time (no credit towards the sentence) and be sent back to prison. He could be paroled again, go back again, and again, and again, creating a revolving door going around and around for a long time. I once supervised a guy in Bridgeport who was sentenced in 1980 to ten years on a drug case and was still on parole twenty years later. Regarding disparity, going from one district to another, or different federal circuits, could be like going from one sovereign nation to another. A guy could get twenty years in Waco on a big drug case, but the same guy in San Francisco could get a split sentence of ten years, with five to serve and five years' probation. These were the two hot potatoes for politicians at the time looking to please their constituents who were looking for tougher laws on crime. It was also during the time of President Reagan's War on Drugs, which he declared on October 14, 1982.

The SRA established the formation of the United States Sentencing Commission (USSC), tasked with developing sentencing guidelines. The USSC became a think tank with judges, attorneys,

academics, and probation officers, who spent three years studying 10,000 cases to create guidelines for a "heartland" of cases
with similar circumstances warranting sentences within a certain
range. Quite a monumental task, which was trumped by two major events: on June 19, 1986, Len Bias collapsed and died. He was
one of the greatest college basketball players of all time and had
just been drafted by the Boston Celtics. It was determined that he
had died from a cocaine overdose and that he had smoked crack
cocaine, which had just been born into the drug world. Thereafter, the Anti-Drug Abuse Act was enacted on October 17, 1986. It
created mandatory minimum penalties for drug offenses based on
the quantity. Crack cocaine was primarily showing up on the East
Coast. It was easy to make and easy to sell. Smoking the rock form
of cocaine rocked the consumers, as inhaling the drug allowed it
to enter the system much more rapidly than by sniffing or snorting
the drug. The hot market for crack on the streets of the inner cities
created an increase of violence and firearms between competitors
who were often rival gangs. The law created a 100:1 ratio, thereby
making the penalties for crack 100 times more severe than for
powder cocaine. Consequently, the USSC had to write guidelines
that incorporated these quantities and related mandatory minimum terms, but they couldn't base the guidelines on the research
and empirical evidence they were developing. I don't know but
imagine that some politician said something like, "I know, let's
make the penalties for crack one hundred times worse than powder cocaine! Yeah, let's do that." The crack was in the inner cities,
and so the law had a familiar, disproportionate traumatic impact
on Blacks and Latinos.

I took to this stuff. It was complicated, and I poured myself
into it. In 1992, before we moved back east, I did a temporary
duty assignment at the USSC on the Hotline, fielding questions
from judges, law clerks, attorneys, and probation officers. As the
independent, impartial advisor to the court, I was determined to
become an expert on the Guidelines. They pay you more money if
you can master that level, and so I was promoted to a Guidelines
Specialist position in 1998. The Guidelines went into effect on

October 1, 1987. But they weren't *really* guidelines. They were laws and were quickly deemed unconstitutional on the District and Circuit court levels based on a violation of one's 6th Amendment rights to due process. Under the Guidelines, sentencing was like a mini-trial, even though the standard was a preponderance of the evidence (51%-more likely than not) rather than beyond a reasonable doubt (let's say 99.5%) required at a jury trial. Approximately six months later, the Supreme Court ruled that there was no 6th Amendment problem (that decision would be reversed in 2007) and away we go! The Guidelines reinforced for me what I already believed in - the power of the written word, sometimes just a single word, even the smallest of words.

When I give Guidelines training to my fellow officers, I like to start by declaring that the most powerful word in the entire Federal Sentencing Guideline Manual is the word "*as.*" For example, say someone is charged with ten counts of bank fraud, each count resulting in a $1,000 loss; they can plea to one count or go to trial and be found guilty on just one count but still be responsible for the full amount of loss. They could be only charged with the one count, but still be responsible for the $10,000. The same principle could be applied in a drug case where someone is convicted on one count charging the distribution of 500 grams of crack, which provides for a mandatory minimum sentence of ten years to life. At sentencing, under the Guidelines, the judge could find that a defendant moved 5 kilos of crack and his guideline range is 30 years to life. The judge just needs to make the finding that the loss or drug quantity is part of the same course of conduct or common scheme or plan *as* the offense of conviction. The essence of the Guidelines is the concept of the "real offense vs. the charged offense" in determining the seriousness of the actual conduct. And there are sentences of course that are legally definitive. For example, regarding disputed facts, of which there are many, the Guidelines state that the court must find that there is " . . . a sufficient indicia of reliability to support its probable accuracy." Just read that to yourself a few times . . .

Probable Accuracy is a great oxymoron!

Chapter 6

Livin' La Vida Loca

TEE BALL IS A big mistake, at least for Jesse. He's a six-year-old spinning top. I try to help him with his focus by teaching him to play chess.

Chess With Jesse

His energy,
a pure wired flow,
gives you a chance
to be a great dad every day
by answering just one question,
"Hey dad you want to wrestle?"
I hope I always said yes
but wish I'd let him win
once in a while.
On the fields of football and lacrosse,
this skinny seven-year-old
has already shown his sharp vision
and sense of angles.
You think he needs
the structure
that can tame
this twirling
whirling dervish,

this pacing cub.
You teach him board positions
and the basic moves.
An easy lesson
with the King and Queen,
the Rooks and Knights and Bishops
and Pawns up front
for protection,
just lines and angles,
counting spaces
with strategy:
Just two or three moves at a time
at first
anticipate your opponent's moves,
don't just react.
He learns quickly.
The board stays
on the kitchen table.
And we play.
A game can take a week, or two.
Jesse makes a move
then starts spinning around the kitchen
his shoulder-length hair
whipping around,
spinning and spinning
and whipping brown hair
"Jess it's your move.
Jess. Jess. Jess it's your move!"
Spinning until still,
for a small moment,
to make a move
before turning and spinning
around and around and around
I am a simple player
moving my mind over the board,
two or, at the most, three moves ahead.
But he teaches me a new game.
I marvel at the motion,
a meditation,
the spinning top,
whirling hair,

around the table,
the kitchen,
the dining room.
He folds time
into a timeless space
returns to the board
makes a move, says
"Your move."
until I no can no longer see
the board, the pieces, the spaces,
only my spinning boy, whirling,
whipping brown hair
leaving and returning
to the pieces on the board,
makes a move
"Dad, checkmate."

He's like a Sufi Whirling Dervish chess master child prodigy from Istanbul. I still can't beat him. So Tee Ball's not his thing. He can't keep still and wait for the play. He's a southpaw, which is an advantage at the plate. I played baseball until I was 19 and love the game, but he needs more action . . . and so it goes. That fall we put him in the Shelton Flag Football League, a hybrid between tackle and flag where the players are in full pads. At the end of the first day of practice Jess comes off the field and says, "Dad, I don't think football's my game." Numberless, priceless teaching moment response: "Jess, we talked about this, and you said you wanted to play. You don't quit something you start, especially after the first day. Never give up." He plays football through his freshman year in high school, but lacrosse is really his game. He's already spent his entire lifetime practicing his stick skills by play sword-fighting with his friends and his father. I don't know much about lacrosse but remember my brief introduction to the sport when I was entering my senior year in high school. They were starting a club coached by the football coaches. Coach Schroeder approached me in the gym during the summer weightlifting program, holding this long aluminum pole with a net basket at the end framed in plastic. "Hey Ray, we want you to play lacrosse with us this spring."

"What's lacrosse, Coach?" "Well all we want you to do is run all over the field with this stick and use it to hit the guy with ball anywhere but his balls or the top of his head." I was intrigued but just wanted to play football. I know that lacrosse can be a violent game but I learned it is so much more. It was invented by the Native Americans and could be played over miles of open land. Sometimes it was a war game played to resolve disputes between tribes. Jess plays for ten years. He plays midfield (middie), which is a player who has wheels and runs all over the field playing both offense and defense. The rules are similar to soccer and hockey, in terms of the lines and offside. Jess plays for the next ten years, gets his varsity letter as a sophomore and is ranked in the top 100 for middies in Connecticut. Basketball is also his game, and he plays rec ball through high school and college. All the way up to middle school, his wavy brown hair is shoulder length and flies in the breeze as he dribbles down court and under the basket before passing the ball. It takes him a while to become confident in his shot. His coach is often yelling at Jess to "Shoot!" when he has a shot. But once he gets over it, *"forget about it."* We have a basketball hoop on the driveway, and he practices all the time.

The five-year age difference between Tebb and Jess sets them up for a wonderfully close relationship during the next several years, until Jesse gets into sports. Tebb loves her little brother, and Jess adores his big sister. They love spending time together, and Jess worships Tebb. From the time he's up and running and string-ing short sentences together, he's often heard calling out "Tee, Tee!" to get her attention. And she is more than happy to pour into him. They spend hours upon hours together, creating characters, co-writing stories, composing music on the computer, and playing video games like *Zelda* and *Kingdom Hearts*.

Tebb is very much a loner and marches to the beat of her own drummer. She is bold and brave. In first grade she performs a piano solo at an assembly in front of the entire school with parents in attendance. She plays all the correct notes. She studies Tae Kwon Do, and during a demonstration at another assembly, she catches an especially hard board and repeatedly tries to break it with punch after punch with the determination of an Olympic athlete trying to break a world record. She doesn't break the board, but so impresses all in attendance by her sheer determination that she receives more attention than she would have had she broken it on the first strike. She doesn't quit. She doesn't give up. In the third grade she jumps into a pool off a ten-meter diving platform. She loves horror and writes a number of very scary short stories about angels and demons and ghouls. In the third grade she also gets involved in Odyssey of the Mind, an international creative problem-solving competition, involving short- and long-term time challenges, the latter involving playwriting, set and costume design, and music . . . all written and created by the team members with no adult assistance. Tebb is the leader of her team and does most of the storytelling. The team goes to the world championships twice and stays together through the seventh grade. It dissolves in the eighth grade.

It is a dynamic and challenging time. Paula is trying to build her program, get tenure and be a mother and wife. The tenure track is a family affair requiring spouse participation. I have to join her at holiday parties and university events. I'm okay once I get there. I usually end up focusing on one person and doing a complete personal and family background interview without their actual awareness of what's going on. I'm naturally inquisitive but prefer to talk about myself. Plus through work, I've met plenty of interesting characters and have a lot of good stories. I even tell an occasional joke, like the one I heard from Judge Squatrito in Hartford. "What do you call an attorney with an IQ of 50? 'Your honor.'" Over time I develop a theory about academics that I call the Cerebral Black Hole. This goes beyond the eccentric, absent-minded professor. An academic's brain becomes so absorbed with knowledge that a black hole emerges in the center which begins sucking the gray matter into an alternate universe. I forget who I hear this joke from, which self-deprecating scholar (a rarity), but I learn what the degrees BS, MS, and PhD mean: bullshit, more shit, piled high and deep.

But when Paula is home and receives the Holy Spirit supernatural energy she needs, she loves us all unconditionally. She reads the *Harry Potter* books to the kids every night that she is home. She scratches my back. She doesn't ask for much in return. One of her love languages is service, so if I empty the dishwasher, do some laundry and put my clothes away, I am the golden man. Unfortunately, I don't stay gold for very long and don't do nearly enough laundry. It is a simpler time. All I have to do with Jesse is wrestle, and when he becomes a teenager and our wrestling becomes a little risky for our bones and the furniture, we water wrestle in the pool. Tebb and I can talk books, movies, and music. We do some things right raising our kids, like teaching about the love of Jesus and exposing them to Classic Rock. But, as in every story, people grow older, things change.

Chapter 7

Back to Bridgeport

AT THE END OF 1999 my chief tells me that I can return to Bridgeport as my duty station, but I must be writing my reports in WordPerfect within six months. Or else what? No worries. It's time to change. I'm *The Last of the Mohicans* as far as dictation goes, at least within the Judicial Branch of government, which I refer to as the Other Branch of government to dispel any animosity directed my way when angry anti-government types understand that I'm a Fed. I always look for the irony in life. It's a literary perspective, or so I imagine. At some point in my career, I realize that I once rebelled *against* 'the man,' and now I *am* 'the man.'

The misconception about my dictation is that I'm computer illiterate. I get this from my colleagues and my family, and I try to explain that it's not true. I use email, do legal research and look up cases online. It's just that I enjoy dictation. It makes me feel special because not everyone can do it. I learn that I am a victim of my own self-deception as far as the writing process is concerned. Like my parents and their parents, Baby Boomers learned to write through a tactile and visual process. You took pencil in hand, placed it on the paper and drew letters, staying within the lines. Letters became words, words became sentences, and so it goes. In high school some took up typing, a higher level of this tactile, cognitive process. Doing dictation is a free flowing, liberating writing process. I am not bound by a desk or a computer. I can walk around my office and write while looking out the window. Well, I am sort of bound to my desk by the documents of my investigation, my source of information: police reports, psych evals, medical records, treatment summaries, my own notes. Okay, so it's not that magical a process, but I like it. I've learned to see the words, sentences, paragraphs, pages, all in my mind.

It's still about speed for me. I was the fastest kid on the block and on the baseball and football fields. I was addicted to amphetamines. But the keyboard scares me. I don't know how to type. This is going to slow me down. Writing in WordPerfect is a revelation, and I become a much better writer. I learn that your fingers will find the keys in your mind's memory. I am a two-to-three-finger typist, and it's fine. As I write this book my fingers are flying well enough. And it's better to see my words on the page than in my mind. I can write shorter sentences. Better sentences. Yes. And that's good. I can see what the reader will see as I write it.

Many great writers have advised that to become a great writer, you need to read great writing. Now Hemingway is certainly a controversial figure in literature, a misogynist drunk who blew his brains out with a shotgun. Most literary scholars and notable writers acknowledge his mastery of the craft. I thought he was famous for saying that a ten-word sentence is the perfect sentence, but that's not true. He did say, "All you have to do is write one true sentence." And that was certainly the goal of writing a presentence report, to write as many true sentences as possible and qualify the others, where appropriate, as reliable hearsay and one's own personal evaluation of what you have learned. I am fond of two sentences I wrote in one report, particularly the second sentence consisting of five words. "The defendant's wife said that she told him if he got arrested one more time, she would leave him. He did and she did."

I become a great editor of my own work. And in the end, it is much faster. I once gave the tape to a clerk, who would transcribe it and return it to me as a very rough draft. I would edit the hard copy, give it back to the clerk, get it back, make more changes, give it back, get it back, and so it goes. Now I just write it, edit, and send it to my supervisor in less than half the time. Enough said. During my five years in the New Haven office, I trained at Montenari Brothers' Gold's Gym. After I transfer back to Bridgeport, I return to the Stratford Athletic Club. I've been training and competing with Flynn's Gym (not an actual gym; just a state of mind) throughout this time. I pay my membership fee, go to train one day shortly after and find the place locked with no forwarding address. This is the world of the fitness club industry. So it's time to start training at South Side Gym. In addition to the equipment, South Side offers an edgy and sometimes dangerous environment. There are lots of guys using steroids, and unnatural testosterone levels are overflowing. I train during off-hours, lunchtime during the week, so there aren't a lot of guys in the gym. But the ones who are there keep me focused on my surroundings in-between sets, when I *check my six*.

Gary is a biker. I think he's a failed Diablos prospect. He's about 6'2", 260 lbs. with a beer gut. I believe he's demonized, if not possessed. He runs around the gym like a mountain gorilla in a zoo and has no idea what he's doing. He hears voices and responds. God gives me Grace, and I spend time with Gary. In the name of Jesus, I command the enemy to flee and pray for him and his ten-year-old son, who he sometimes brings into the gym. Gary ended up catching a federal gun case and going to prison.

Brother Jerry is from Mt. Vernon, New York. He sold drugs in his early 20s, caught a felony case and did a year in the Westchester County Jail. He was angry all the time and ready to explode. Over the years I was able to share God's Word with Jerry, and he finally found his way to a place of peace. God wrote these verses on Jerry's heart. "In your anger do not sin: Do not let the sun go down while you are still angry, and do not give the devil a foothold." Ephesians 4: 26, 27

" . . . be quick to listen, slow to speak and slow to become angry, because human anger does not bring about the righteousness that God desires." James 1: 19, 20

We remain close brothers in Christ.

To the casual observer, powerlifting would appear as a very strange thing. It attracts a wide variety of people. I meet a lot of cops, criminals, blue-collar and white-collar guys, even some academics. I'm still training and competing in the gear and have about 25 meets under my belt. I stay right around 235 lbs. body weight for 15 years, toward the top of the 242-lb division. I never have to cut weight, which can be a torturous journey. I bench 400 lbs. in 1998, and leading up to 2000, my best squat is 640 lbs., deadlift 680 and total is 1,685. The gear gets crazy down the road. I still have a big black hefty bag full of old powerlifting suits in my basement somewhere. Today people can increase their bench by 300 lbs. and their squat by over 400. It's absolutely insane. In my last full competition at Iron Island in Long Beach in March 2000, I put up a 1,670 total and win best lifter. After that my shoulders start grinding out loud with each rep. I decide to get it checked out and go to the Yale Sports Medicine Clinic. I'm looking at the x-ray of my shoulders with the resident, and he explains that the dark lines are the cartilage, which should be a quarter-inch thick. He points out that my cartilage looks like a line made with a pencil. "So, doc, how would you compare my shoulders to a 65-year-old?" The Doc replies, "Try an 80-year-old." And so it goes. My full meet days are over, but this frees me to concentrate on my deadlift. More importantly, in October of that year Paula gets tenure, and this frees me from my academic spousal duties.

"Submit to on another out of reference to Christ." Ephesians 5:21

Chapter 8

9/11

I'M IN THE FIELD that Tuesday morning in the government car doing a home visit in Danbury with a guy who pled guilty to a conspiracy to traffic in counterfeit currency. Dan is a middle-aged, single white male with no kids, living alone in his deceased parents' home. It's a fairly large case in which he worked with a younger Latino woman with excellent computer skills. They sold thousands of dollars in counterfeit twenties to some Latin Kings from the Bronx. It's a jail case. I've got the mobile phone with me, which is a corded phone and base station weighing about five pounds. We are years away from getting our BlackBerrys. If you can't call 911 quick enough you can always use it as a weapon.

Dan is a strange guy. He claims to be a black belt in Tae Kwon Do and a trainer for the Danbury Police Department. He gives me a tour of the large Victorian house that was built around the turn of the 20th century. It looks like he's a borderline hoarder with stacks of books, magazines, tools, clothes, and knick knacks piled throughout the home, which is otherwise unkempt and in need of a good cleaning. The lawn needs mowing, and it doesn't look like any landscaping has been done in over a decade. During every home visit you reach a point when you know it's time to go. I am nearing that point when Dan shows me his father's World War II service medals, including a Bronze Star and Purple Heart. He's got his father's DD-214 in one hand, the federal indictment in the other, and starts getting teary eyed as he laments over the shock reverberating in his mind from when he heard the charges read out in Court: "The United States of America v. Dan John." He is ashamed of himself and knows his father, the war hero, must be rolling over in his grave.

It's 9:00 am when my phone rings. It's my coworker Mike Guglielmo telling me that some nut case just flew a plane into the World Trade Center. "Ok Dan. I need to get back to the office. We'll talk soon." As I walk toward the car, I look up and appreciate the clear blue sky and think, *what a great day for some lunatic to fly into a building.* I hope there aren't too many people injured. It's just another crazy day in Metropolis. I'm in the car driving back to Bridgeport on Route 25 when Paula calls. She's hysterical and can't put a sentence together. I tell her I'll call her back when I get to the office in about 25 minutes. All I can think is that my mother-in-law died. I couldn't have known that my mother had called Paula to tell her to put on the T.V., and together they watched in terror as hijacked jet, Flight 175, flew into the second tower at 9:03.

I get back to the federal courthouse in Bridgeport in time to see the South Tower collapse at 9:59 and the North Tower go down at 10:28. We start to understand that it's a massive terrorist plot involving Al Qaida, and there might be other targets such as courthouses, train stations, and schools. The courthouse remains open until 4:00 pm that day. I can't understand why.

Tebben starts noticing that her fourth-grade classmates and other students are being called down to the principal's office, starting first thing in the morning and continuing throughout the day. She overhears teachers in the hallway talking quietly about terrorists and the possibility of schools being attacked. She is angry with the terrorists and angry with her parents for not coming for her. Paula picks up Tebben and Jesse after school and brings them home. She's been sitting in front of the television all day watching the horror, speaking with family on the phone and crying. I try unsuccessfully to get a hold of my buddy, Steve DeLuca, who's a New York City firefighter. It's a week before I find out he's ok.

Kingdom Bound gets invited to sing in front of the Trumbull City Hall that Friday at noon. There are a few thousand people there. The healing has already begun all over the country. We sing *America the Beautiful* a cappella, followed by *God Bless the U.S.A.* by Lee Greenwood, which will become the new national anthem in the weeks and months to follow. There are some federal clerks at the gathering. Word gets around and Kingdom Bound starts singing at naturalization and award ceremonies. After the group breaks up a few years later, I keep singing patriotic songs at these events. Judge Stefan Underhill organizes the 9/11 ten-year memorial in front of the federal courthouse in Bridgeport. I sing the *The Star-Spangled Banner* and *Where Were You When the World Stopped Turning* by Alan Jackson. After that, Jeff Bingham from the IRS joins me with his acoustic guitar and backup vocals, and we are the band until retirement and beyond. This is just a small change in my life after 9/11.

We are still "America Divided," but for the next few months we come together. Love overcomes our fear and prejudices. We are united. We look each other in the eyes. We talk to strangers. We pray in public. We are changed, but the love doesn't last. We remember what happened, the death toll, where we were and whom we were with. We remember how it made us feel, but not how we felt toward each other. That is but a vapor a mist.

"Why, you do not even know what will happen tomorrow. What is your life? You are a mist that appears for a little while and then vanishes." James 4:14

Chapter 9

Stroke

WEIGHTLIFTING HAS ALWAYS BEEN a blessing in my life, but competitive powerlifting lifts me to a higher level. I've been consistently deadlifting over 600 lbs. since I was thirty. I've weighed around 230 for the past ten years. My best meet total is 1,685 lbs., and my deadlifts in the mid-to-upper-600 range having placed me on the Powerlifting USA Top 100 and Top 20 Master lists several times, earning me some state, national, and world records for old guys. But eventually with bone-on-bone in both shoulders, I'm resigned to competing only in the deadlift. It's fine. It's my strongest lift, and my training becomes more focused. In July 2002, I pull 685 lbs. to set a state record at an American Powerlifting Association meet in Norwich, Connecticut. God is giving me great strength, physically and mentally, and that's good because I will need it in the years to come.

The morning of January 14, 2003, my sister Teresa calls Mom, and they discuss dinner plans later that night for her daughter Danielle's 20th birthday. Danielle is Teresa's oldest of three daughters. Later that afternoon, Mom and Dad settle into their adjacent offices on the west side of their ranch home. Joe Cavetano, my parents' all-around handyman, is working on the in-law apartment on the opposite side of the house. Dad is on his computer running tests on his latest equation, and Mom is writing an email to a contractor who did a shitty job on a shelving unit and won't provide a refund. She's angry.

Mom's about to hit send with her right index finger when her hand drops onto the keyboard and fate stabs a knife through her brain. She tries to stand up but can't. She tries to call out but can't. When she falls, Dad hears a loud thump in her office and runs in to find her on the floor. He calls out to Joe to call 911. The ambulance arrives within 20 minutes. While they wait, Dad calls the ER at Huntington Hospital and speaks with Mom's best friend, Noni Greising, so they are ready for Mom when they get there. Noni and Mom have been working together in the ER as RNs for the past 35 years. They have seen it all. But not this.

Dad calls Teresa and tells her they are on the way to the hospital. She leaves work, and within minutes she finds herself driving right behind Dad in his new red Jeep Grand Cherokee. Mom bought it for him for his birthday last November. Approximately 45 minutes after suffering her stroke, Mom receives tPA, a drug that can treat a stroke by breaking up the blood clot. It has proven to be highly successful when given within less than an hour after the stroke. I'm probably halfway over the Throgs Neck Bridge by this time; my youngest brother, Pete, is coming down from Richmond, Massachusetts, and the middle boy, Steve, drives straight through the night from Cleveland and arrives at the hospital just before sunrise. Teresa is the oldest. We don't realize it just yet, but God's mercy and grace abounds. Dad is partially deaf and still struggles to hear with the best hearing aid money can buy. Had he been in the kitchen down the hall, he never would've heard Mom's fall and she could've laid there on the floor for hours. The treating physician at the ER advises Teresa and Dad that Mom's prognosis is poor, and she might end up on a respirator. He must be a new intern because he obviously doesn't know how tough Mom is.

She's asleep when I get to her room that night. She looks peaceful. She's beautiful. Then she opens her eyes.

Stroke

Such a soft word.
Such a hard truth.
As you lay in silence
your heart
reaches through
your eyes,
your smile,
your tears.
I softly stroke
your hand,
your face.
And I remember
each moment,
how you gently stroked
my soul
when I was a baby,
a boy,
a man.
This stroke
took you down.
I never noticed
how soft is your skin
and your hair
until now.
And I think of this
Journey
we must take
and thank God
for you
for each stroke
of your hair,
your face,
your hand
I hold like a child
as a man
afraid to let go.

Mom is released from Huntington Hospital after a few days and transferred to Saint Charles Rehabilitation Hospital in Port Jefferson. The stroke left her unable to speak and with limited use of her right arm and leg. At Saint Charles she is programmed for physical, speech, and occupational therapy. Teresa is the art director at Amana Tools in nearby Farmington and can see Mom every day during her lunch break. I take the ferry over when I can to visit. On one visit I find Mom in bed. Her eyes are pouring out love. I pick her up in my arms, which gives her a thrill. She knows I'm strong, but it's still exciting for her and she smiles and giggles like a little girl. I place her in a wheelchair and start rolling her around the hospital when we run into Teresa. She tells me that Mom hasn't had a bowel movement in a few days, and her stomach is starting to swell. The hospital wants to discharge her because she's not making progress in therapy. But Teresa is as tough as mom and tells the staff that they need to address Mom's medical issues. During the second week, she takes time off from work and camps out in Mom's room. At the end of the week, Mom is discharged and takes another ride with the Commack Volunteer Ambulance Corp back home. She is one of their most precious passengers, one of its founding members.

Teresa is there every day after work to help Dad out. Mom is receiving a regular dosage of physical therapy, speech therapy, and occupational therapy. She is digging in and making a dogged effort, but it's hard on Dad. Mom needs help with showering, going to the bathroom, getting dressed, daily hygiene—essentially everything that needs to be done. Dad and Teresa quickly realize they need help, and Teresa starts to search for a 24/7 home health aide. She sets up interviews and people come through, but Mom doesn't like any of them. She is struggling with her new reality and the idea that someone will be living in her house. It is her worst nightmare. Teresa becomes exasperated and finally says, "Mom, if you don't accept this, I'm going to have to quit my job and leave my family to stay here and care for you!" They cried in concert many times, and eventually Rusa becomes part of the family. Rusa is originally from the former Soviet State of Georgia. She is a strong, sturdy woman who has been through a lot. Her green eyes reflect her courage and love and so it goes. Rusa has a daughter back in Georgia and a worthless, abusive ex-husband. She is paid well and sends money back to Georgia. She hopes to bring her daughter to the United States. And one day she does.

The therapy is going well. Mom starts getting around, at first with a walker and then just a cane. The speech therapy is tough. It is hard for her to form the sounds of the alphabet, but she can clearly say "he." This word becomes her voice, and with her body language, especially her eyes, she communicates. But it can be extremely frustrating and exhausting when there is a failed communication. After several attempts at Q & A and exasperated, Mom exhales deeply and looks down. There is anguish, but she keeps fighting.

Within a year, they find a tumor in Mom's pituitary gland. They have to surgically remove it by going through her nasal cavity. After the surgery it's clear that the tumor wasn't the only thing gone from Mom's life. Her drive and determination to come back is severely diminished. She is still a force. Her "he-hes" express all her emotions: her love, her desires, her joy, her sadness, her insistence, her energy and fatigue. Her voice, coupled with the expression in her eyes, commands attention. She settles in and eventually, over the next several years, stops her therapy and becomes non-ambulatory.

Chapter 10

Practicing Prophecy

IN 2005 GOD RELEASES us from Long Hill. Like in every church, there are problems. Mahatma Ghandi once said, "I like your Christ, I do not like your Christians. Your Christians are so unlike Christ." The leadership at Long Hill is in alignment with the Southern Baptist Convention and woman aren't recognized as leaders, but for Children's Church, fundraisers, and potlucks. Paula is not only a Christian woman of strong faith but also a scholar who studies the Bible vigorously. She finds many examples of strong women in leadership of the church. There's Deborah, Esther, Tamar, and the noble wife in Proverbs 31 in the Old Testament and Lydia, Susannah, and Mary of Magdalene in the New Testament. We stayed because I believed that God wanted me to serve and evangelize through the quartet, Kingdom Bound; Paula, a Proverbs 31 wife, stands by her man.

She meets with the pastor many times to discuss God's word about women in leadership, but her understanding is not appreciated. Now women were allowed to give a testimony before services, but when Paula takes the opportunity to share a message God gives her titled "Jesus, the First Feminist," the walls begin to come down.

We've been at the Huntington Chapel in Shelton, Connecticut, for a few months, and a prophet named David Wagner is visiting the church for the first time. He comes from Jubilee, a large

church in Southern Florida, a man of average height with short
dark black hair, dark brown eyes that look deep. After serving in
the Baptist church for 15 years, I know how to share the Gospel
and lead others to Christ. I knew I was an evangelist the moment
I accepted the Lord through a baptism of the Holy Spirit. I know
little about the gift of prophecy but read a lot about false prophets
in the Bible. I'm skeptical to say the least.

The Body is moving in open corporate prayer, about 100
brothers and sisters free in the Spirit to pray as one feels led. Powerful, passionate, some cry out, some pray softly, some pray in
the Spirit in a language of their own, a gift from God. It moves in
waves, at times rising to a crescendo of many voices, then crashing
to the shore of a single voice. Pastor Doug preaches on prophecy,
a word of knowledge, in which God reveals a piece of your past
through one with a prophetic gift to bring healing or a word of
wisdom to reveal his plan for your future. David starts pacing back
and forth across the front of the church calling forward those who
want to hear a word from the Lord. I kneel in the middle of the
room. I'm not moving. I'm good right there, where God planted
me, knowing He heard my prayers, the body heard my prayers,
on my knees, eyes closed, rocking back and forth as the worship
team plays.

I hear David moving through the body, praying and speaking words over people. He pauses for a moment. People pray and
cry out, "Thank you Jesus, Hallelujah, thank you Jesus, thank you
Lord." I feel a hand on the top of my head, then David's voice, a
subtle Southern drawl, but sharp in tone: "Evangelist, evangelist,
evangelist." I think *so what, big deal, he heard me pray.* Anyone
who heard my prayer would know I am an evangelist. I've been
working as a federal probation officer since 1990 and often pray
for my cases—mobsters, gang members, addicts. Then God speaks
through David, "You have been through the School of Hard
Knocks," and I know I'm hearing the voice of God through this
man. That refrain of my life, spoken by my earthly father, again
and again. I fell down on my face. I know it's real. God is speaking
through this man. He speaks through David and says, "You will

evangelize the hardcore, one at a time." My plan and vision as an evangelist is sharing my testimony in an auditorium filled with the lost who would rush forward after hearing me speak to receive God's gift of salvation. God knows my prideful heart and calls me out on it right there on the floor of the Huntington Chapel, and my life as an evangelist becomes just as He plans, the hardcore, a condition of the soul, one at a time.

I know that "There are different kinds of gifts, but the same Spirit distributes them . . . To one there is given through the Spirit a message of wisdom, to another a message of knowledge by means of the same Spirit, to another faith by the same Spirit, to another gifts of healing by that one Spirit, to another miraculous powers, to another prophecy . . . " 1 Corinthians 12:4–10. But the Apostle Paul invites us all to prophesy — "Therefore my brothers and sisters, be eager to prophesy . . . " 1 Corinthians 14:39.

We are motivated to pursue the gift of prophecy so quickly after our encounter with David Wagner. Elder Vincent Carbone and I attend a teaching on prophecy by Jan Nel, a powerful prophet from Johannesburg. We hear strong testimonies from Jan, and he teaches that you must have faith, be bold and not give in to the spirit of fear, not to worry about failure. It's something you can practice. So as an evangelist I have learned to hear from God and go for it without hesitation. Many times, I tried to evangelize in my own strength and approached individuals God did not call me to minister to. Toward the end of the session, Jan invites us into a time of prayer and meditation, to hear God's voice and receive a prophetic word for someone in our group.

I look around the room and find myself drawn to a young man in his early 20s. I see that his heart has been broken many times and hear that God has allowed that pain to occur to equip this man to minister to others and help them receive their healing through faith; God has been preparing him, this entire time of suffering, to be strengthened and prepared to receive the wife He has chosen for him. Wow. I am excited.

The next part of Jan's teaching is to invite someone to give the prophetic word they received. I am not afraid (maybe just a little) and am the first to stand up and volunteer. I approach the one God chose, and it's like performance art and poetry as I share the prophetic word given to me. Now we know we must test the things of the Spirit; God instructs us to do so. After my eloquent offering of the gift, Jan asks the gentleman to comment on the accuracy of what he heard, and he responds with "Absolutely none of that is even close to being accurate." Praise the Lord. I thank God for the gift of evangelism and need to practice, real hard, pursuing the gift of prophecy. And humility. As a probation officer, although prohibited by the authority, I have many opportunities to bring the love of Christ to others. When doing a personal and family history interview, there are certain questions, in my opinion, that must always be asked, for example: "Did you have any religious upbringing or experience? And do you hear voices?" I've conducted many interviews when, after responding that they have no history of mental or emotional problems, the person responds in the affirmative after I ask in the negative, "That means you've never heard voices or had hallucinations, right?" If during the course of the interview, someone shared that they were raised Christian or had converted to Christianity, I immediately felt released to explore that experience deeper and to share scripture and move in the prophetic if possible at the end of the interview.

Now in the federal system it is almost considered malpractice if a defense attorney isn't present during the presentence interview, as anything a defendant says could be used to determine his guideline range and the probation officer's recommendation. I believe I have God's covering, but I need to move carefully. In terms of moving in the prophetic, I just spent anywhere from one to three hours talking to someone who has shared with me all the details of their life. I'm not likely to get a word of knowledge, but if I really pay attention to the spiritual realm, I can be open to receive a word of wisdom.

If someone offers that they read the Bible, I would always ask what verses speak to them or what their favorite verses are. This can open many doors. God provided me with three verses during my career that I would often offer at the end of an interview.

Romans 8:28 says, "And we know that in all things God works for the good of those who love him, who have been called according to his purpose." Many people I investigate are career criminals with files that weigh five pounds. I would hold up the file for emphasis and again say that "God means what he says and when he says all things, he means all things, even this, everything in your file. But most of this wasn't done according to God's purpose."

While this is going on I remain aware of my surroundings. What's the attorney doing, reading a newspaper, taking notes, listening intently? "You see there are three plans for your life: God's plan, your plan, and the enemy's plan. We've already agreed that you haven't been entirely following God's plan. Now sometimes we can come up with our own plan that looks pretty good. We have strengths and talents and can put those toward a good purpose, but if it isn't part of God's plan it usually doesn't work out as we hoped. And the enemy's plan is simply to lie, cheat and steal in order to destroy you, to kill you." How's the attorney looking right now?

God covers me. At the end of one interview during such a discussion, a federal defender, who is now a magistrate judge, interrupted to let me know that she thought what I was trying to do was totally inappropriate and unprofessional. Another defense attorney came back to my office after his client left to tell me that there was something different about me and wanted to know what it was. He then poured out his soul and we prayed together. Philippians 1:6 says " . . . being confident of this I am certain, that he who began a good work in you will carry it on until the day of Christ Jesus." Put simply, God's not done with you. And to bring us home, one of my favorite power verses, I'm declaring that "I can do all things through Christ who strengthens me." Philippians 4:13. "When God says all things, he means all things: the good, the bad and the ugly."

I keep trying to hear God's voice in the prophetic and keep my eyes and ears open to be ready for the moments. Sometimes it's but a whisper and applying to a small thing, and sometimes it's huge and relates to major life-changing events. During the summer after his freshman year, our son, Jesse, is at an unsupervised party and becomes dangerously drunk. The father of his good friend brings him home to us, in spite of Jesse's pleas to let him sleep over their house, which was the original plan. I walk/carry Jesse into the house, help him take a shower, then put him to bed, hoping he will have such a horrible hangover the next morning that he will never drink again. Paula doesn't agree with this strategy, and we take Jess to the ER, where he is given an IV (and a diagnosis of alcohol poisoning), which saves him from such suffering. We have a family meeting the next day after he's released from the hospital, and Jess tells us he's sorry that he scared us, he didn't like the sense of losing control and promises he will never disappoint us like that again.

The next weekend we all take the ferry to Long Island to visit family. I seize the opportunity to prophesy into my own son's life. I tell him that God allowed him to have a glimpse of his future if he ever drinks again, that he is just like me, wired for addiction. I was wrong. He's not an alcoholic. We ground Jess for the summer, and he takes thousands of jump shots on our driveway court. One day I grab 500 consecutive rebounds for him. His shot improves dramatically, a bright and shining silver lining.

"For faith is the substance of things hoped for, the evidence of things unseen." Hebrews 11:1

Chapter 11

Angels and Demons

GOD HAS USED THE Huntington Chapel for decades as a "Holy Spirit Hospital." The broken will come, receive Christ or renew their faith and relationship and be healed. Some leave thereafter, others stay, but always when they come, they experience the love of God through his people. Worship is the primary power of the Chapel. It is always moving, flowing through a storm, a song, a whisper, a prayer. It lifts us up and slays us down. It breaks off chains and builds armor. It releases tongues, interpretations, and prophetic words of knowledge and wisdom. We sing, cry out and remain still in His almighty power.

But like any church gathering, some are not feeling it, receiving it, or so it may seem. There are families, generations, children, teens. Many adolescents are there because they have to be. Their parents made them go. For my own children, I'm grateful that they honor us by attending. And even though they sit, silent, as if in the middle of the eye of a storm, oblivious, God can be working in miraculous ways. Tebben is 13 when we begin going to the Chapel. God has given her many gifts, but the most precious of those is her eye, her ability to see the light and shadows, the movements and colors of the world of the supernatural—revealing His intimate Glory.

Tebb doesn't sing or dance, she doesn't pray out loud. She sketches in her pad, especially during worship. One morning I look and see that she has drawn an epic battle between angels and demons, and when I look through her pad, I see dozens of images of these scenes, taking place in heaven, on the streets, or in the Chapel itself. We talk and Tebb simply explains that this is what she sees during worship when she closes her eyes. The images just come, and she just draws. And I hear God saying that he's given her the gift of discernment.

In 1 Corinthians 12:8–10, God teaches that "[t]o one there is given through the Spirit a message of wisdom, to another a message of knowledge by means of the same Spirit, to another faith by the same Spirit, to another gifts of healing by that one Spirit, to another miraculous powers, to another prophecy, to another distinguishing between spirits . . . " Paula and I pray into it.

People start noticing Tebb's sketching during worship and start asking to see what she has drawn. Many are moved by the images they see. Some feel a direct connection to their own circumstances and receive what God has for them. It is awesome. He has given her the gift. When facilitating a service, I sometimes call out the teenagers, usually Jesse and the Carbone boys in the back row, but mostly I leave them alone. I leave it to God.

It's amazing how different we are, how unique and wonderfully made by God. His children, even those raised in the same environment—the same home—-will grow and respond differently. Like our children: there is a five-year age difference between the two and when they were younger, they spent all their time together. Tebben adored Jesse, and he worshipped her. Love is a resounding bell that echoes when we grow apart, a river running endlessly but changing over time. Jesse is a homebody. He would be perfectly content to stay home and be with his friends. If we never went anywhere as a family, he'd be a happy camper. Tebb has wanderlust. She decides to take a gap year after graduating from high school and travel to Ecuador to live and work for a women's cooperative in Quito. I say to Paula, "We're not letting her go, right?" Paula and Tebben don't skip a beat. Shortly after her 18th birthday, we find ourselves in the International Terminal at JFK waiting with Tebben before she boards a flight to Medellin, with a destination of Quito.

It's like a dream in which I'm wrestling with faith and fear. I know where both come from. I don't want to let her go. This little girl who used to run up to me and throw herself into my arms when I came home from work is about to board a plane destined for the equator. Only passengers are allowed through TSA, but I manage to persuade a supervisor to let me escort Tebben to the gate after showing him my shiny badge. We walk to the gate. Tebb has always had a determined, powerful stride, like she knows where she's going and what she's going to do, like a Spartan marching into battle. I watch as she disappears through the gate, and I pray.

"Therefore, since we are surrounded by such a great cloud of witnesses let us throw off everything that hinders us and the sin that so easily entangles." Hebrews 12:1

Tebben's sketch

Chapter 12

Rich

I MEET RICH MACCHAROLI at the Stratford Athletic Club when he joins the Flynn's Gym powerlifting team at the beginning of 2002. We become lifelong friends for far too short a time. Rich is about 5'6" and 150 lbs., an accomplished martial artist with a 3rd degree black belt in Tai Kwon Do and a black belt in Brazilian Jujitsu. He's from Lordship, Connecticut, where he is a local legend for some unavoidable fights. Rich has whooped bullies twice his size.

When I meet Rich he is going through a bad time. He just got laid off from his job as a welder at Avco Lycoming, where he worked for 15 years before Avco was sold to Textron. He also just went through a horrible divorce after 15 years of marriage. His ex-wife had an affair with his best friend. He got joint custody of his young daughter and son but lost his house. Martial Arts saved his life and kept him off the streets, but now he needs more stress release, and powerlifting seems like a gift from God.

Powerlifting is tough and hard to stay with. That's why it's almost an underground sport. Flynn's Gym eventually disbands, and Rich and I are the only two members still training. Now, I have known Rich's father, Nick Maccharoli, aka "Batso," for years, as he was one of the original Flynn's Gym members. Nick is unforgettable. He is a famous auto body guy who is tattooed over 90% of his body. He designed some award-winning custom cars, like the King Tut Mobile, and has played bit roles in movies and mini-series like

Oz on HBO. Nick's devoted wife, Elly, is 27 years younger. She takes good care of him and keeps him going. Nick is an outspoken exhibitionist, and Rich is quiet and humble.

I share my faith with Rich, and he shares his story of great disappointment in God. His mother was a devout Born Again Baptist and took Rich and his older brother, Michael, to church. She battled with cancer for several years before she died when Rich was 12. Nick was angry the entire time she suffered and took it out on his sons, physically and emotionally. Rich doesn't want to hear about Christ. And so it goes.

We train hard at South Side Gym and spend a lot of time together. We get our kids together on occasion and grow to know and love each other. We do some out-of-the- box medieval training. I'm still competing in the deadlift and cycling up for an American Powerlifting Association meet in Norwich one summer. We spend six weeks in our yard loading up a wheelbarrow with huge stones from the wetlands behind the house. We take turns pushing the wheelbarrow about one-and-a-half acres to build a stone wall for Paula's garden. As a result, in July 2002, I pull a new Connecticut State Record 685-lb. deadlift in the Masters 242 lb. division. It was the hard work born through our partnership. I couldn't have done it alone.

We meet at South Side one day for a squat workout in the summer of 2004. We start stretching, and Rich starts talking about how his right leg feels weak. I tell him "No worries, you're just tired; we'll go light today." And so it goes. Rich's right leg gets progressively weaker. The doctors can't figure it out. We keep training. He lets me pray for his healing. Eventually, Rich starts using a cane to get around. We keep training, and I keep praying. Rich's left leg continues to weaken, and he moves from a cane to a walker. We keep training; I keep praying, and the doctors still can't figure it out.

About a year after it starts, Rich calls me one day and asks if he can come over. We had a hard workout earlier in the day, so I suggest we go in the spa. He arrives and we're hanging out, and he tells me the doctors finally came to a diagnosis—ALS, Lou

Gehrig's disease. Rich is afraid. He starts to cry. It's the first time we pray together.

Rich starts using a wheelchair to get around. I pick him up and we go to South Side and train. He trains his upper body. The disease starts working its way into Rich's upper torso, and he's no longer able to work out. He moves in with his girlfriend, Suzanne, who lives in a condo complex about three miles from our house.

Rich has no assets or income and qualifies for Title 19. He's set up for home health care at the condo with a hospital bed in the living room. I see him every morning for a few minutes on my way to work. He still has some use of his arms and has no speech impairment. His mind is clear, and his heart is full. I walk in the room and Rich is up, glad to see me, ready to talk about what's going on in my life and with our kids. He's full of light. And when I come and when I go, he raises his left arm to say hello, shake my hand and bid me a good day. As the days and weeks and months go by, I start to notice that his arm is raised a little lower, and lower, and lower, until he can't move his arms at all. But Rich is a fighter, and I keep praying for a healing.

ALS keeps attacking Rich's body. His doctor says that he's in perfect health, but for his ALS! Rich's needs increase every day as he loses his ability to care for himself. Suzanne does the best she can. When I visit, I sometimes feed him and help Rich to the bathroom, but as he approaches being non-ambulatory, he is placed in Connecticut Hospice in Branford. It's a beautiful facility very peaceful. I don't get to see Rich as much but visit whenever I'm in New Haven.

He's still fighting. He wants to believe. He's Full Code so when he's in distress they take him to Yale New Haven Hospital. As ALS continues its attack, Rich comes under respiratory distress quite often and ends up in the ICU at Yale. I'm praying for Rich one afternoon in the ICU when I feel the Holy Spirit pressing on my heart, and I know I have to invite Rich into the Kingdom. He's ready and accepts Christ into his heart. And he becomes a new man in the midst of the great irony of his life. He was able to do things with his body that most people couldn't imagine. Now his

body is his enemy, his prison. But he never complains. He brings "
. . . beauty instead of ashes . . . joy instead of mourning . . ." Isaiah
61:3. He's on a mission from God to love everyone and make sure
they're ok. A couple of times we gather at hospice, possibly for the
end. But Rich keeps fighting on.

They move Rich to a rehab facility in Waterbury. It's not a
great place. I guess his time just ran out at Connecticut Hospice.
Most of the nurses are caring, but some shouldn't be working there.
Our good buddy Joey Solano and I see Rich every Tuesday night.
We have a routine. We try to make him comfortable, and I read the
Bible and pray. One night we find Rich in a state of high vexation.
We can smell the problem the minute we walk into his room. He's
been lying in his own shit for who knows how long.

We now use about 100 index cards to try to communicate
with Rich, every conceivable question from scratching his ass to
adjusting his feeding tube. He can still move his head up and down
for yes, and side-to-side for no.

One night during a torrential downpour, Joey and I arrive to
find that our friend can no longer move his head. We have no idea
how we're going to communicate with him. So I do the only thing
I know to do; I pray. I pray that the Lord helps us to communicate
with Rich and understand what he needs. As I'm praying, a male
nurse enters the room. He's starting his shift. He starts working
with Rich and asks him if he can blink his eyes. Rich blinks. He
tells Rich to blink once for yes and twice for no. And so it goes. I
love when God provides an immediate answer to prayer.

Joey and I return to the car to head home. It's still raining
cats and dogs. I know Joey was raised Catholic, but I don't know
if he has a relationship with Christ. The harder it rains, the more
I feel released. "You know, Joey, we can check out of this world at
any time, on a night like tonight while driving home." I know he's
listening; I can feel that he's ready. "You know heaven and hell are
real places, and God has given us the choice. Christ died for our
sins so we can be with him in heaven." Joey tells me he believes, but
he's never asked Christ to come into his life. It's a beautiful thing.
I ask Joey if he wants to pray with me. He says yes. I ask him to

repeat a simple salvation prayer and he is saved, or so I hope. We sit in the silence of the rain beating down on the roof of the car, and Joey sees my doubting heart through the Holy Spirit and says, "Ray. I meant it."

Rich's body keeps shutting down, and he's in and out of the ICU at St. Mary's Hospital in Waterbury almost every other day. He's still Full Code but Nick and Elly, Rich's stepmother, are his health care proxies. The only saving grace is that he gets excellent care in ICU. On January 10, 2007, Joey and I visit Rich at St. Mary's. The ventilator is breathing for him now. His eyes roll back, and we pray for him for the last time. Nick and Elly come later that night, make the decision to take him off life support, and Rich leaves this world to be with Christ. Thereafter, every time I'm having a rough day, feeling frustrated, angry, impatient, depressed, I think about Rich, and I'm convicted once again. God placed Rich in my life for a reason, for things yet to come.

"Do everything without grumbling or arguing so that you may be blameless and pure, 'children of God without fault in this crooked and depraved generation.'" Philippians 2:14

Rich throwing a spinning roundhouse kick. Rich was about 5'6". His sensei was about 6'4".

Chapter 13

One at a Time

GOD INSTRUCTED ME TO witness to the hardcore, one at a time. What's hardcore? It's easy to see in the physical realm but in the spiritual, not so easy. Remember that Satan appears as an Angel of Light.

On most days of the week, I drive to the office in Bridgeport. I take Route 8 South, get off, make a right onto Fairfield Avenue, a left on West Street, a left on State Street, and the courthouse is right there. There's a bodega on the corner of Fairfield and West and a park across the street. It's a very active spot. There's drug trafficking, prostitution, and homelessness. And there's Poppo (it takes me two years to learn his name). Every day he's out on the corner just standing there, taking it all in. He's a short Hispanic man with dark-brown weathered skin, a nice round face and dark-brown eyes that look deep. He appears to be in his mid-60s. We make eye contact every time I drive by; I mean *really* make eye contact. Not a quick glance and turn away but a straight stare saying *Okay, I see you*. This goes on for two years! We never speak. I never stop. But each day we stare. Eventually we make progress in our communication and exchange slight head nods of respect.

Toward the end of the second year, after I begin pursuing the prophetic, I start feeling a tightness in my gut as I drive by, a sense of guilt and anxiety. It's the conviction of the Holy Spirit. I know that God has a word for Poppo, and I must trust and obey. Each day it becomes harder to drive by without stopping. I start to dread turning that corner. One day in the office I tell my coworker and Christian sister, Jane Castaldo, about Poppo and tell her that I'm planning on pulling over to talk to him the next day. She understandably cautions me because of the criminal activity at that spot. I tell her that I understand, but I have to stop, and I ask her to be praying for me tomorrow morning.

When I pull to the side of the curb the next morning, Poppo is looking in a roll-off trash bin behind the bodega. The corner is crowded with people as usual. When he sees me pull over and get out of my car, I can see the fear in his eyes as I approach. I'm dressed in my typical shirt and tie, although my personal policy is to never wear a white shirt. I may be 'the man' but that doesn't mean I have to look like the man! Anyway, I suspect that he thinks I'm a cop because he begins backing away from me.

I start with, "Hi. I know we see each other almost every day, but I had to stop because God put it on my heart to pray for you." He seems to relax and stops stepping backward. The first sign that God's plan is working is that Poppo speaks good English, *porque yo hablo Español un paquito solamente. Entendio más que hablo.* So here we go, just Poppo, God, and me.

I ask Poppo if I can pray for him, and he says yes. I ask him if there's anything he needs prayer for, and he says no. I ask him if I can place my hand on his shoulder as we pray, and he says yes. And I start praying. As I pray for a blessing over his life, I feel God telling me to place my hand over his heart. And as I continue to pray, I feel there's pain in his heart, and I pause and say, "I feel God wants me to pray over your heart, that you have a heart condition that brings on fear and causes you anxiety." Poppo's eyes suddenly get bigger as he begins to tell me about his history of heart problems and the surgeries he's had, including the stent that was just recently replaced. And we both rejoice. I pray for God to heal his heart and take away all his fears. Poppo shares his story about his Polish wife; how they got divorced because she was tough and always yelling at him. He tells me about his two adult children, his son, who lives in Hartford and is a contractor, and his daughter, who is a teacher in New Haven. I learn that Poppo is retired after working in the maintenance department for the City of Bridgeport for 30 years. He lives in an apartment over the bodega and knows everyone on the corner. He tries to help people and looks out for those most in need, like the prostitutes and the homeless.

Thus begins our relationship, slow at first but steady as we go. I try to stop every morning I'm going into the office. I speak to the storeowner and learn that Poppo has been living above the bodega for the past 20 years. Everybody knows Poppo and even refer to the spot as Poppo's Corner. I share my testimonies and faith with Poppo and he makes an affirmation of faith in Christ. I start bringing a box of Dunkin' Donuts coffee every morning so he can offer coffee to the people on the corner.

I see a change in Poppo. When I come by, he is no longer standing around and staring, but he's talking to people. After a while Poppo asks me if I have any Spanish Bibles that he can give to those who need one. A holy non-coincidence, there is a box of Spanish Bibles that's been sitting at the Chapel since we've been there. I also find a bunch of English Bibles and Spanish and English Bible tracks.

Poppo's corner ministry goes on for about two years. Sometimes he introduces me to people and asks if I can pray for them. He must shut it down during the winter, but he's back the first day of spring. One new spring day I see that Poppo is not on the corner. For the next two weeks he's not there. I finally stop and go into the bodega. The owner tells me that Poppo died over the winter from heart failure. He adds that everyone expected him to go a few years ago, as he was constantly in and out of the hospital, but the last couple of years he was healthy and happy, always giving people coffee, praying for people and handing out Bibles. My sadness lasts but a small moment and then my heart rejoices. I share Poppo's testimony at the Chapel and in the office and pray that I can see who God has for me next.

John Wood is the president of the Shelton Flag Football League and the meanest man in town. He's controlling, demeaning, uncompromising, disrespectful, and foulmouthed. He gave our son's coach a hard time for letting Paula be the team statistician because she's a woman. He works as the vice-president of a custom floor company. One day he came home from work, got upset because his youngest son didn't bring in the empty garbage cans, and kicked the family dog, breaking its ribs.

I've been a coach in the league since my son was seven. He's now 14 and wants to play tackle football in a new American Youth Football (AYF) team in Shelton. I tell Kevin Scanlon, the head coach of our team, that I'm taking Jesse out of the league to allow him to play AYF, so Kevin can advise John at the next coaches meeting. Kevin gets back to me to share the flurry of expletives John used in expressing his opinion about what a big mistake I'm making. About a week later, I get a voice message on my cell phone from John, "Hi Ray. It's John. When Kevin told me you were leaving the league my heart sank. Ray, I've been watching you over the years interact with the kids, their families, and the coaches in the league. There's something different about you. I've always wanted to talk to you and ask you about it, and when I heard you were leaving, I thought I lost my opportunity. Would you please give me call? I would very much appreciate it." I play the message for Paula, and we are both in a state of disbelief. I don't believe it. I think it's a ruse so John can tell me what an idiot I am for leaving the league. But I know I need to call him. I feel I owe him that.

The next Saturday, a hot August day, I grab the phone and tell Paula that I'm going out on the back deck to call John Wood. He picks up and essentially starts repeating what he said in his message. He tells me that he knows I'm a Christian and just sees me as a kind of light, especially when I'm with the kids. He tells me he was raised Catholic but when John was 18, his father died, and he became angry and disinterested in religion. As John continued to pour his heart out over the phone, I looked at Paula inside the kitchen and mouthed the letters O-M-G. And I felt like laughing out loud. I felt like God was laughing with me, having a little fun with me, and teaching me what *He* means by hardcore. There John was, right in front of me, out on the field. A middle-class, married white male with a wife and five children. He wasn't a drug-addicted homeless guy sleeping under an overpass, or a made Mafioso, or a white-collar fraudster, or a gang-banging drug dealer. He was the VP of a company and the president of the league. I invited John to the men's prayer meeting at the Chapel on Saturday morning and ended the call by praying for him and his family. Then I told Paula, and it's the first time that God baptized me with the Holy Spirit in laughter. We both started laughing with joy. It felt so good. God is so good, all the time. He laughed with us.

And God's timing is perfect. John starts going to men's prayer and attending services at the Chapel. I keep him in my prayers during the week and usually call him once a day when I read scripture that I think is applicable to his life at the moment and just to check in. John eventually starts attending services at the Chapel and brings his wife, Kyra, a few times. The change is startling to those who don't understand what's happening to him. He is kind and considerate. He doesn't curse and has stopped drinking. And he listens. After around six months, I see John sitting in the back of the sanctuary one Sunday morning during a service, and I see that he's undone. He is sobbing deeply, with his head down and his hands covering his face. I mean deep heaving sobs, like waves during a storm. I sit down next to him and put my arm around his shoulder and wait. The Holy Spirit storm subsides, and the new John Wood looks into my eyes. I see a new light, a new joy. John shares that he just accepted Christ right there on that pew in the back of the sanctuary in the Huntington Chapel.

You hear people often say that God doesn't give us more than we can handle, and that's true as long as we're living according to his plan and purpose for our lives.

1 Corinthians 10:13 says that "No temptation has overcome you except what is common to mankind. And God is faithful: God will not let you to be tempted beyond what you can bear. But when you are tempted, he will also provide a way so that you can endure it." The spirit of addiction has been attacking John's son, Nick, for quite some time. A few months after John gets saved, Nick is out shooting up heroin with his buddies. They're driving around when Nick stops breathing. His friends drive to the nearest ER, drop him

off on the curb outside the entrance and drive off. He is flatlining. By the Mercy and Grace of the Lord, a nurse inside sees what just happened, and Nick is quickly taken into the ER. Like Lazarus, they bring him back from the dead.

God has prepared John for such a time as this. He loves his wife and children into the Kingdom. Nick makes a full recovery and uses the powerful testimony God has given him to minister to those wrestling with addiction. John has always had the gift of leadership but now uses it for God's purpose. He becomes a leader in a local men's ministry and impacts the lives of hundreds of men. He is the new John Wood, and forever I have this testimony to share.

"And they overcame him by the blood of the Lamb and by the word of their testimony; and they loved not their lives unto the death." Revelation 12:11 KJV

Chapter 14

First Death

THE DAYS ARE LONG but the years are short. Mom fights valiantly to stay involved in the lives of her family and friends. She goes to her grandchildren's sporting and school events on Long Island, where she sits in her wheelchair on the sidelines and shouts "he he" to celebrate their accomplishments. It's amazing what she communicates with that sound. Sometimes it's like a soft song, so soothing to our souls, and sometimes it's like a sharp knife, piercing our psyches as we share in her pain. Her voice in combination with her eyes and facial expressions tell us what we need to know and what we can't imagine. My favorite thing is just to sit with her on the couch and hold hands. And Mom and Dad continue having Wednesday nights with the girls. They've been getting together for years with Mom's closest friends and nurses from the ER: Noni Greising, Kathy Stark, and Judy Tenzycki.

Rusa has been a blessing to our family, but it is time for her to leave. Her daughter and young grandson have come to the U.S. from Georgia, and she is no longer able to provide Mom with the care that she needs. She leaves in early June 2010, and Leisha arrives at the end of the month. She is there during the weekdays and off on weekends.

The care falls mainly on Teresa, who helps Mom shower. She has been non-ambulatory for a few years and has been sleeping on the couch/recliner in the living room since that time. I am able to provide relief over the weekends. Mom has gotten heavier during her years of inactivity, so my physical strength from a lifetime of heavy lifting comes into use. She ain't heavy. She's my mother.

She's hanging in there. She's there to meet her first great-granddaughter, Deanna, who is born on May 20, 2010. When they first met in my parents' living room, Mom's eyes got bright, her "he hes" sang a song of love, and I thought she was going to stand up out of her chair!

Toward the end of August 2010, I arrive in Commack early Saturday morning to spend the weekend. They are all in the living room: Dad, Teresa, Uncle George, and Mom. For the last few months, Mom has been in and out of the hospital, a day or two here and there. She had just come home the day before. Everyone is looking exhausted, but I am ready to go.

I sit down next to Mom and give her the tiny pink dumbbell to do some curls. She smiles and "he hes" exasperatingly. The visiting nurse comes for a follow up, and when she's told that Mom hasn't urinated since being home, she advises that Mom needs a catheter but that has to be done at the hospital. My family sinks into sadness and fatigue and lament that she just came home. I look at Mom and announce, "I've got it. We've got it right, Mom?" I get a "he he," in a solid tone of agreement and off we go.

Mom gets special treatment at the ER. She is a living legend there, and there's a plaque in her honor hanging on the wall. She gets to cut the line; we are in a room, and the catheter is put in in no time. Then we just have a good time. There's a drug-addicted patient across the hall trying to get some opioids. There's a fist-fight in the lobby requiring security, police, and an arrest. It's just another day in the ER. We're in and out in four hours. Before we leave, I help Mom with her matching earrings and necklace, a basic black, white, and yellow beads with a yellow heart at the bottom of the necklace. When I go to put it around Mom's neck, she starts "he heing" and points at my neck, indicating that she wants me to have it. I put it on and later hang it from my rear view mirror where it still hangs today. We have a great weekend.

Before I head home, I go to Dad's study and ask if I can pray for him. I've been doing this all summer. He is always receptive to prayer. Our spiritual journey together has been a long one, going back over 30 years, when I first accepted Christ.

Early on, I tried to evangelize my parents. During one long drive home with Mom after visiting family in Ohio, I gave her my full-length testimony and asked if she wanted to accept Christ. She declined in love. After a decade or so of sharing my faith with Dad, he straight out told me how happy he is for me and he doesn't want to hear the Gospel anymore. God worked on us all.

A few years after Mom's stroke, she told me she believed in Jesus as her Lord and Savior. And Dad began his own spiritual journey after Mom's stroke. His lifelong philosophy, his trinity if you will, evolved from mind, body, and personality to mind, body, and spirit expressed through love. He eventually said to me, "Ray, I've come to accept my parents' religion. For me it's Christ, but I'm not going around telling anyone else what they should believe." "That's great, Dad. I'm so happy for you and no worries, I don't believe God's calling you to be an evangelist anyway." So as I get ready to pray for us before I leave, Dad says to me, "You know Ray, I also pray to God." "That's great Dad. I'm so happy to hear that." "I pray that he takes your mother home, so she doesn't have to suffer anymore." "That's alright, Dad. That's a good prayer. Let's pray together."

Mom's brother, George, had moved back east to be with his sister from LA, his home of many? years. It was a roller-coaster of a time when everyone's love for Mom manifested in a tumult of extreme, sometimes excruciating emotions. But God breaks through — always — if we have ears to hear and eyes to see. Uncle George tells us that the week before when he was in the kitchen and Mom was on the couch dozing, he heard her laughing. He goes to investigate and finds her asleep with laughter softly trickling from a peaceful smile. Paula and I are convinced it is a meet-cute with Jesus.

"Jesus said to her, 'Everyone who drinks of this water will be thirsty again, but those who drink of the water that I will give them will never be thirsty. The water that I will give will become in them a spring of water gushing up to eternal life.' The woman said to him, 'Sir, give me this water, so that I may never be thirsty'" John 4:13–15

Two weeks later, on the evening of September 4, 2010, Mom lets Dad know that she wants to go to bed. She hasn't slept in their bedroom for a few years. Early the next morning, Teresa calls me and tells me that Mom passed away sometime during the early morning of September 5. She knew it was time to go and wanted to sleep one last time with Dad. After we hang up, I feel a shift in the universe, in my heart and mind, a new pain, a loss. Lost in a new wilderness, dark foreboding woods, I wander through the towering pines, seeking the light. This lasts forever and about 15 minutes when Heaven opens enough for me to receive that peace that surpasses all understanding, and I feel the arms of Christ around her, that eternal embrace, and I rejoice. I tell Paula that Mom is with the Lord, and I'm driving to Commack.

When I arrive, I find Dad, Teresa, and Uncle George in the kitchen. We hold each other's hands and pray. Mom isn't there. We all feel her love and peace in our grief. Two men from the funeral home arrive to take away the body. I go into the bedroom with them and watch as they place the body in the black bag and zip it up. I escort the body to the van parked in the driveway and watch them drive away. I am the watchman, the head of the family. I need to be strong. I give the eulogy at Mom's memorial service. It's the hardest and easiest thing I've done in my life. There is so much to say about her love and her life. My parents have known each other for 70 years and were coming up on their 57th wedding anniversary in December.

I tell some funny stories. Like one Saturday afternoon, I was shooting pool for money with some friends. A primary rule of my residency as the beast in the basement: I couldn't leave my shit upstairs, especially my shoes. As I lined up the winning shot, the basement door opened, and Mom threw my boots down the stairs. They hit the end of the cue stick, causing me to scratch on the shot and lose the game. My friends started laughing and I got pissed off, picked up the boots, and launched them up the stairs, smashing against the door. The door opened and Mom slowly descended the steps. I leaned back against the end of the pool table, the cue stick in my hands, trying to be cool in front of my friends. She swiftly grabbed the stick and smacked me over the head several times, rendering me stunned and seeing stars; she then placed the stick back in my hands, which helped me maintain my balance as she ascended the stairs. My friends followed her up silently and exited through the back door. Thereafter, any time I invited people to come over to party or shoot pool, they always asked, "Is your mom going to be home?"

I talk about Mom's imprisonment in her own body and imagine out loud how she must be talking God's ear off, sharing with him all the things she wanted to say to us for the past several years. In summarizing Mom's life, I end with 2 Timothy 4: 7,8: "I have fought the good fight, I have finished the race, I have kept the faith. Now there is in store for me the crown of righteousness, which the Lord, the righteous Judge, will award to me on that day—and not only to me, but also to all who have longed for his appearing." I have to evangelize, if only in a subtle, loving way. After I finish, I sit down and start to cry and tremble. Tebben sits down beside me and puts her arm around my shoulders. Then she walks up to the podium and shares some memories she has of Mom from when Tebb was a young girl, like nestling up against her and feeling the smooth softness of her periwinkle blue silk shirt. It's poetry.

We're getting ready to leave the funeral home when and old friend, Brendan Smith, walks into the room. I haven't seen Brendan in over 20 years. He was one of the guys in the basement playing pool that day. He tells me he had no idea Mom had passed. After he got home from work, he sat down to read the paper and saw her obituary. He jumped in his car and raced to the funeral home. We catch up. Brendan has cancer. I lay hands on him and pray for his healing before we leave. He died from cancer a few years later.

We have another ceremony the next week at the cemetery where we intern Mom's ashes. It's a small gathering: Jim and Jenny St Pierre, my parents' good friends and next-door neighbors,

Paula, my siblings, and all our children. I offer a short message of hope and end with prayer. Dad puts Mom's ashes in place and cries. It is the first and last time I ever see him cry.

"There are also heavenly bodies and there are earthly bodies; but the splendor of the heavenly bodies is one kind, and the splendor of the earthly bodies is another. The sun has one kind of splendor, the moon another and the stars another, and star differs from star in splendor. So it will be with the resurrection of the dead. The body that is perishable, it is raised imperishable; it is sown in dishonor, it is raised in glory; it is sown in weakness, it is raised in power; it is sown a natural body, it is raised a spiritual body." 1 Corinthians 15:40–44

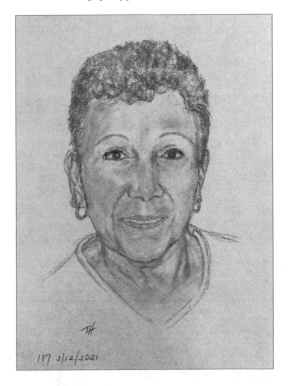

Teresa' Sketch of Mom

Chapter 15

God Speaks

GOD SPEAKS TO US through the glory of nature, the power of his written word, world events, and one another. He spoke audibly to Adam and Eve, Noah, Moses, Abraham, Isaac, Jacob, Deborah, Mary, Joseph and Paul, just to name a few. And he still speaks audibly. He speaks to me. Over the years he has spoken to me three times, all within the last several years.

I've struggled at times being an evangelist; witnessing in my own strength when it wasn't in God's plans, being prideful about my testimony, missing clear opportunities and suffering conviction of the Holy Spirit, and not praying that God show me the lost.

Insomnia has plagued me in my latter years and at times sunk me into depression. It's after 3:00 one morning, and I'm trying to get some sleep. I need to sleep as I am running my first unit meeting in the morning as a supervisor. I'm meditating on God's Word, inhale " . . . be still . . . " exhale, inhale " . . . be still . . . " exhale, inhale, " . . . be still . . . " It's starting to work as I feel myself slipping into the void, when I hear "3:19" in a loud, deep, masculine voice. I immediately open my eyes, feel the hair rise on the back of my neck, my heart burns with adrenaline and fear. I turn to my left and see that the digital clock on my nightstand shows 3:19. I sit upright. I know it's God. I'm thinking scripture.

I've been reading my Bible straight through, cover-to-cover, continuously since we've been at the Huntington Chapel. I started with a daily devotional, first on my knees praying every morning for a half hour. Then a chapter, write down the meaning after the first read; read it again to receive what God has specifically for me; then a third time seeking the direct application to my life, or someone else's. I did this for six months until my calves started to cramp badly, which I took as a sign from God that it was time for me to get off my knees. But during this time, God gave me dozens of verses to memorize by writing them down and repeating them. Sometimes I received immediate memorization. And each time, whether it was the next day, the next week, or months away, I found myself in a situation where one of those verses spoke directly to the circumstances.

I don't know 3:19, or which book, chapter or verse I should check. I think about John 3:16. A multitude of folks know that verse, even non-Christians, especially baseball fans, because they've seen it so often they looked it up. "For God so loved the world that he gave his only son, so that whosoever shall believeth in him shall not perish but have everlasting life." Then I know where to go. Why didn't I know John 3:19, or 17 or 18 for that matter? Well I can paraphrase 17 and 18. I open my Bible to John 3:19, "This is the verdict. Light has come into the world but men loved the darkness instead of the light because their deeds were evil."

And my world changes in that small moment as an evangelist. I have to remind myself, every day, that it's a matter of life and death. I have to open my eyes to see whom I can see in the spiritual realm. I have to open my ears to hear God's voice.

The second time I hear God's audible voice, I'm at a retreat for the probation department being held at a beachfront hotel in Rhode Island. It's late at night; I'm in bed and watching crap on TV. I turn off the television, and I think about an old girlfriend and masturbate. And I feel the conviction of the Holy Spirit. It's not just spiritual but also physical. I feel a tightening in my gut, heaviness on my heart.

I'm lying there suffering when I hear a soft male voice say, "Hey Ray." And that's it. It's a simple moment with my friend Jesus. He's just checking in with me. He knows my heart. He knows my mind. I know that lusting after another is committing adultery in your heart, the same thing in God's eyes as if you had done it in the flesh. Jimmy Carter was all over this in his Playboy interview, in which he admitted that he struggled with lust. I don't understand it. I don't need to understand it. I just know I'm good. God just gave me a head nod and a "Hey Ray," and I know I can do better.

The third time God spoke to me was after my mandatory retirement from Federal Probation following my 57th birthday. Most folks don't know that all federal law enforcement officers are met with this same fate. You sign up for it at the start and as you get older, the days are longer and the years are shorter until you're there before you know.

Some people do 20 and out at 50. They're made to retire—naturals. I would've stayed. I loved my job. Retirement was hard. The one thing that helped me find balance was volunteering at St. Vincent's Hospital in Bridgeport. The goal was to visit every new patient. Three days a week, I'd arrive at the Pastoral Care Office to pick up my list of new patients to visit. I'd walk in an accessible room and say "Hi. My name is Ray Lopez and I'm from spiritual care. We try to visit every new patient to see if we can help you in any way and to try to get to know you a little. Would you like a visit?" Some folks would politely decline, and others would invite me in. I'd ask them background questions about their lives, explaining that the hospital staff usually knows about one's medical history and current status, but not much else. My notes from the visit would go into the electronic record and be accessible to the doctors and nurses. Knowing more about their patients would enhance the care provided, or something like that. It sounds good, right?

At the end of a successful visit, I would ask if the patient would like to pray and to offer anything they needed prayer for besides the obvious. I volunteered at St. V's for about two years. I prayed for a lot of people, from the elderly getting close to the finish, to the young men all shot up from gang violence. God used me to lead some into his Kingdom, but mostly it was just praying for healing and family.

One afternoon I'm walking out after a few intense hours. It's late and there's no one around. I'm exhausted. Halfway down the hall I hear that same voice, only a little louder and energetic, say, "Good job." And I'm just walking out feeling blessed, feeling his presence, *knowing* I did a good job.

Chapter 16

Three Weeks in Peru

IT'S A BEAUTIFUL DAY in Fairfield County, Connecticut, on July 13, 2016: bright sunshine, clear blue sky and not a cloud to behold. It reminds me of when the world stopped turning on September 11, 2001. Now this might seem like a trite beginning to this story, even with the ironic reference to 9/11, but to use some well-worn clichés, the truth is stranger than fiction and it shall set you free. Miracles are strange, extraordinary, but also a simple matter of faith as small as a mustard seed.

I'm a month from retirement. Tebben has been living and working in Peru for 18 months. She just turned 25, and Jesse is turning 20 in August. He's about to start a new job in the produce section of ShopRite. I surprise Paula after work that day by showing up for her graduate information session on campus. I know there'll be free food and beverages. We get home around 8:00 that night, and I'm getting ready to barbeque when I notice a missed a call on WhatsApp from Vivian Baca Smith, one of Tebb's housemates. My heart pauses for a small moment, and I tell Paula I'm calling Vivian back.

Vivian informs me that Tebb has been hit by a bus and is in Cuzco at Clínica Pardo. Tebb was in a meeting at a cervecería in Pachar, a small town in the Andes about 10 minutes from Ollantaytambo (Ollanta), where she has been living and working for Awamaki, a small non-profit that supports women artisans from the local indigenous Indian villages. She was with her friend, Jason Grover, an ex-Marine who had done a couple of tours in Iraq. He's been struggling with his PTSD and has been sober for six months.

We're all action; on the phone with Blue Cross/Blue Shield, conferencing with the clinic in Cusco. Paula is up all night booking a flight to Lima. All action. Teresa and my niece, Jacqueline, drive out from Long Island to be with us and drive us to the airport early the next morning.

We're strong. We have a team. Vivian books us a hotel down the street from the hospital, Clínica Anglo Americana.

When we reach a time where there's nothing else to do, at that moment, I feel the fracture in my heart, the pain and anguish. A baby cannot cry like a grown man.

God also puts it on my heart to fast until Tebben wakes up. We know that family and friends expect the worst. There's no judgment from us, only love and understanding. Tebben was hit by a bus; another common cliché: "It could be worse. At least you didn't get hit by a bus." We have prayed our entire lives together for this moment. We have a choice and choose faith.

Through Social Media (Facebook and group texts), hundreds of people begin to pray.

July 13, 2016 Post from Vivian:

"After hit she was in and out for 10–15 min. once they put her in the ambulance she was unconscious. She has a compound arm fracture. She wasn't bleeding a ton it was a head wound. Our landlord Juan knows the owner of the clinic and all the best doctors have been briefed on her condition. She's getting a cat scan right now and we're waiting for her to finish the scan. our friend Michelle a very experienced PA from the USA is with her in the scan."

Tebben suffered a fractured skull, a compound fracture of her right wrist, a fractured pelvis and three broken ribs, all on the right side of her body. She and Jason had just gotten out of their meeting at approximately 5:00 pm. Tebben crossed the street (single lanes in each direction) and was waiting at the bus stop (as you can see from the photo below, this stop is just an elbow in the road against the side of a huge rock). Jason was on the opposite side of the road and had negotiated with a cab driver to take them back to Ollanta. He waved to Tebben to cross the street to the cab parked in the opposite lane. At the moment Tebben stepped onto the road to cross, a tourist bus swerved to the left to avoid hitting a car. The driver saw Tebb at the last minute and slammed on his brakes . . . too late to avoid hitting her.

After being struck, she was in and out of consciousness for ten to 15 minutes, spewing forth every curse word known to man. Jason was the first responder, which is the first moment of God's Grace as he was field-trained in first aid and CPR. Another of Tebb's friends, Michelle Glatt, upon hearing about the accident from Joe and Louisa, two of the owners of the cerveceria, called for a private ambulance, knowing local transportation could not make the two-hour drive to Cusco. Michelle is a physician's assistant who works for Sacred Valley Health, a non-profit that trains community health workers living in Andean communities. Michelle rushed to Pachar to find a crowd at the accident scene, but all she could see was Tebben. She jumped into the ambulance as the EMTs lifted Tebb and placed her in the vehicle. The doctor recognized Michelle and nodded his head.

During the entire drive to Cusco, the doctor and Michelle work hard to keep Tebben comfortable, but they are both very worried. They dress the compound fracture to her right wrist, but there isn't much they can do for her head injuries with what was available in the ambulance. Vivian and Michelle were coordinating on the phone during the transport. Michelle knew Tebb needed ID and proof of health insurance, so Vivian went to their house, found Tebb's passport and our contact information, called us and left a message, all before the ambulance arrived in Cusco.

The bus driver and his family showed up at the clinic and stayed the entire time Tebb was there, asking what they could do. The driver was distraught. He had not been under the influence of drugs or alcohol. She was stabilized at the clinic, but they did not have the staff or equipment to treat her injuries. The plan was for her to be airlifted to a hospital in Lima the next day.

The average size tourist that would come through on the way to Machu Pichu.

July 14, 2016 Posts:
"The start of the journey-
The minute Paula and I hear about Tebben's accident we nail our hearts to the Cross, rest in our Faith and know she is safe and will fully recover. We immediately receive the Word from God- Exodus 14:14 and Jeremiah 29:11. It is the hardest and easiest thing we've ever done. Paula has nausea from the start. We get on the plane from Newark to Orlando. I'm sitting between Paula and Sheryl, who's sitting on the aisle seat across from her husband. She is a middle-aged woman and is holding a book with a pamphlet on top titled 'God's Continuing Faithfulness' by Charles Stanley. At that moment, I am struggling with fear and my heart is spiritually and physically broken. When I read these words, God speaks to me and reassures me of his mercy and grace. Sheryl notices that I see the pamphlet and hides it at the back of her novel. I have no idea who she is or what she believes but I know God plans to use her to bless us. About halfway through the flight, I introduce myself, explain our circumstances and tell her that God spoke to me when I saw what she was reading. She and her husband are spirit filled, faithful Christians and she and I share our testimonies, have fellowship and praise the Lord the rest of the flight. As the plane begins to descend, Sheryl says she wants to pray for us. I wake up Paula, who's sleeping and still feeling sick.

Sheryl begins and prays Jeremiah 29:11 into our journey. The instant she begins to pray and call upon the Lord's name, Paula is healed of her nausea. This is how our trip begins (see story of PT John Angeles from time in clinic in Lima, as it pertains to Jeremiah 29:11."

It's a God start.

"For I know the plans I have for you", declares the Lord, "plans to prosper you, and not to harm you, plans to give you a hope and a future." Paula tells me later the reason she could sleep on the plane was because God reassured her with that verse the night before. Sheryl's prayer was a second confirmation that Tebben was in God's capable hands and would survive. The second of many. Jeremiah 29:11 was an anthem of sorts, heralded by angels sent to comfort us during this trial.

In Orlando we transfer to a flight to Lima and arrive in Peru at 10:45 pm. Vivian meets us at the airport. She's the second of the ministering angels we're destined to meet. She tells us that Tebben is still unconscious and was initially given Fentanyl for pain because of the compound fracture. They also started her on a drug that will reduce the brain swelling. The airport's a beehive swarming with people. After we convert some cash into soles, we get into the taxi that Vivian pre-booked. It's like being in a movie, balancing between fear and faith.

It's around midnight, and a radio news broadcast is playing. Vivian interprets and tells us there's been a terrorist attack, and the Eiffel Tower is ablaze. It's of no consequence to us. It's later determined that the Tower caught fire accidentally but was at first thought to be connected to the 19-ton cargo truck that was deliberately driven into crowds of people celebrating Bastille Day on the Promenade des Anglais in Nice, France, that day, resulting in the deaths of 86 people and the injury of 458 others. It was just another day in our new upside-down world.

We arrive at the Grand Hotel Betsy at around 1:00 am on July 15. Tebben would arrive at Clinica Americana later that morning. There's a lot of dogs barking early that morning, as if they sense our fears. We sleep some and for me, the hotel café becomes the weeping place. I am inconsolable, uncontrollable in mind and body, thinking about the moment of impact on her body, her mind, and I weep and sob and feel my heart dissecting, and Paula is strong and somehow never sheds a tear the entire trip. Each morning thereafter that first week, I swim in tears of prayer.

We're met at Clinica Americana by the president and owner of the hospital, a friend of Juan's father, who assures us of the best of care. At 1:45 pm the airlift from Cusco, carrying Tebben, Juan, and Michelle departs for Lima. Juan managed to arrange for a private jet from Cusco to Lima, which was amazing, as they are difficult to come by in rural Peru.

It lands at approximately 3:00 pm and arrives at the clinic an hour later. We see the ambulance from a second-floor lobby window as it pulls up to the emergency room. We run down to the street in time to be there when they remove Tebb from the ambulance. She looks so small and fragile lying on the stretcher, like a baby swaddled in a blanket. She's intubated and has multiple IVs attached, still unconscious. The only visible part of her body is her closed eyes. Paula and I hold each other tight as they wheel our baby into the ER.

As Tebben is swept into the emergency room, we meet Juan and Michelle for the first time. As she enters the ER, Tebb is surrounded by an army of professionals ready to take care of her, and Michelle, who's been on guard the entire time, is overjoyed that Tebb is in a place that can properly care for her injuries. I ask Michelle if we can enter the room to pray. She walks in, asks the treatment team if this was ok and instantly each doctor and nurse put their gloved hands together at their chest and took a giant step backward, giving Paula and I the space to walk right in, lay hands on Tebben and pray. Amazingly, she doesn't look too beat up.

Tebben's placed in the ICU, which has very strict rules on visiting, the first being only one visitor at a time, wearing scrubs and a face mask, the second being very limited visiting hours. They eventually break that rule for us and allow 24-hour access. They make exceptions to a lot of the rules for us, as guided by the Holy Spirit. The hospital is immaculately clean. There are housekeeping staff buzzing around like drones, vacuuming, mopping, and wiping everything down 24/7. This is a good sign. There's a cleansing atmosphere over the hospital, which was founded by British missionaries in the 1920s.

July 15, 2016 Social Media Posts:

"Tebben Gill Lopez is sleeping right now. Initial prognosis is favorable. Spent a powerful time praying over her- praying in the spirit and God's prophetic words over her temple and the atmosphere in her room and this hospital that was founded by British missionaries in the 1920s- 1 Peter 2:24, 2 Corinthians 12:9, Isaiah 40: 29–31, Ezekiel 14:14, Philippians 1:6. Read these verses into your prayers for Tebben.

No bleeding on the brain-swelling going down, no femur break, no internal injuries, breaks all manageable.

She's sleeping- all drugged up because she's agitated, which is good, and they don't want her to stress the breaks, particularly the pelvis.

The sedative, combined with the drug directly involved in reducing the brain swelling have her unconscious but they are reducing the sedative gradually.

The blessings just keep coming. We just met a mother and son outside Tebben's room, who told us that the neurosurgeon who is caring for Tebben has a great healing anointing in addition to his skill and he recently performed a miraculous surgery on a young girl and saves her life. We gave thanks and prayed together for Tebben and their father/husband, a miraculous stroke survivor!

Paula's text: I just spoke to Dr. Hinojosa the neurosurgeon. I was in with Tebb and he came in. What he told me is nothing short of miraculous. He said she has NO bleeding on the brain and NEGLIGIBLE TO NO SWELLING. I asked him three times to clarify but he didn't waver. So the plan is to wean her off the sedative tomorrow so she can wake up, see her status, and figure out next steps. The trick is finding the right meds to allow her to come 'back to reality' while making her comfortable pain-wise. We are now believing specifically for a good pain-free awakening and a good cognitive assessment. So as has been the case, keep your prayers coming. They make all the difference."

A team of prayer warriors is beginning to grow. Our niece, Danielle, sets up a Facebook page; Paula and I start group text messages, and I write numerous public Facebook posts. There will soon be hundreds of people from all over the world following our journey and praying into our trial. Tebben is agitated, fighting the drugs preventing her from placing stress on the fractures, particularly her pelvis.

July 16th was an amazing day. Interchangeably, Paula and I are able to spend five hours with Tebb, most of the time praying in the Spirit and singing hymns and Psalms. Tebben begins to struggle and fight into her healing as they slowly reduced the sedative. During one of my visits, she does a crunch, raising up both knees and lifting her head off the pillow. I see her pain but more the intensity in her face; being healed but in a hurry, inpatient and frustrated, the same Tebben we've always known. Toward the end of that visit, she sits halfway up, opens her eyes and sees me. Praise the Lord! They decide to let Paula and I visit together. At one point, Paula says, "Open your eyes honey," and she immediately responds and looks at us. Later in the evening, when Tebb's once again wrestling with her pain and frustration, she nearly sits upright in bed, and when Paula asks, "Are you in pain?" she nods her head up and down in affirmation. It's hard to watch her suffer and see her frustration but a greater blessing to see more evidence of her healing.

That day we speak with the facial surgeon who examined Tebb. He tells us that she may not need surgery on her right cheek, but he would have to reevaluate in two weeks. He also tells us that her eyes are responding well to light (we have already seen evidence of that) and that she will be evaluated by an ophthalmologist. After he leaves we lay hands on Tebb's face and pray for her complete healing. Every day we lay hands on the injured parts of her body and pray for a healing. Before we leave, the nurses ask Paula if she can stay because they see how well Tebb responds to her.

July 17 and another morning of anguish in my heart and soul. My spirit is willing, but my flesh is weak. I sit in the cafeteria of our hotel and picture Tebben in her hospital bed. I think of the moment of impact when the bus broke her body, and I feel the impact on my heart. I read my Bible and receive: "For God who said, 'Let light come from darkness', made his light shine in our hearts to give us the light of the knowledge of the Glory of God in the face of Christ." 2 Corinthians 4:6. It's the same light spoken into existence that is in us in Christ! Beyond understanding. "For the secret things belong to the Lord our God, but the things revealed belong to us and our children forever." Deuteronomy 29:29

Encouraged, I visit Tebb that afternoon, mostly singing to her. I joke with the prayer warriors on social media about my beautiful voice, which worries me because Tebb might think it was an angel singing to her. Dr. Hinijosa tells Paula that although the X-rays taken in Cuzco showed lesions on her brain, his X-rays show none. He tells us they may wake her up tonight or tomorrow, at which time they will remove the breathing tube and start talking to her to test her cognitive functioning. Then we're alone again. I am overjoyed and say, "Tebb, look at me," and she opens her eyes and looks into mine! She's now basically responding to us and her friends by opening her eyes when someone calls her name and raising her eyebrows as an expression of surprise.

On July 18, Tebben is still coming down from the sedation, so she's in and out of consciousness. They tell us to talk to her, and Paula goes on for hours but especially catches her attention and opens her eyes when she tells her that: She's going to be the next new superhero— TEBBEN, they should get new matching tattoos saying AMAZING GRACE . . . Idris Elba called and he's leaving his wife for her (she actually tries to laugh but still has a breathing tube in so Paula knows she needs to tone it down), She wants to climb into bed with her and watch Tarzan (Tebben smiles), Jesse sends his love and is praying for her, Her eyebrows look great, are her friends Rosanna and Isabel helping her with them?, It's uncle Mich's birthday.

Paula also asks her some yes/no questions which she responds to with nods. She tells her she's a rock star and asks, "Are you feeling me?" She nods yes. She asks if she's surprised to see us; she nods no. Paula also gives her a neurological status exam and she responds accordingly. She tells her to blink, squeeze her hand, nod yes and no. She also has an x-ray taken of her wrist, which means they're getting closer to performing surgery, and they tell us that the breathing tube will be removed the following day.

Paula sends out this message to the hundreds of prayer warriors on vigil: *"Pls keep ur prayers coming. They make all the difference. We're trusting Jesus for a night of supernatural PEACE & REST as she continues to come down off the drugs and they find the right balance for her pain meds. This is her theme verse God gave me that I pray over her constantly. Jeremiah 29:11 'For I know the plans I have for you,' says the Lord, 'plans to prosper you and not harm you, plans to give you hope and a future.' Please join me in this prayerful refrain. love you all."*

Tebben's breathing tube is removed, and she becomes fully engaged . . . talking and understanding what is happening to her and what's going on! Praise the Lord! I sent this message out:

"And these signs will accompany those who believe:" Mark 16:17 Now get this! Tebben was hit by a tourist bus and came away with barely a scratch on her beautiful skin, no brain damage and so far requiring only one operation to repair the compound fracture on her arm. We are witnessing Holy Spirit Wolverine healing through the Blood of Christ—a miracle."

On July 19, Paula spends the morning talking to Tebb. It's hard for her to speak at first because the tube removal left her throat very sore. After a while she understands and answers Paula's questions with yes/no, or repeating what she said. Eventually, they have a conversation: "Do you know who I am?" "You're my mom." (like "duh"). She asks Paula what the box is at the bottom of the bed with all the wires coming out of it and tells her the phone is ringing again (it was one of the machines she was hooked up to). At one point she looks worried because she realizes she was in a bad accident. Paula tells her, "You were asleep for 4–1/2 days, but you're 500% better than when you arrived in Lima and 200% better than yesterday and 100% better then when we came in this morning till now. I promise you're going to be perfect again soon." Tebben replies, "I'm so happy to hear that."

We have to leave Tebb's bedside because the nurse comes to prep her for surgery. We spent most of the day with her. It was a great day but as she became more aware, the realization of what happened settled in and caused her to be a bit discouraged. We ask for prayers of encouragement and hope. Her wrist starts to hurt her badly at one point so the surgery can't come soon enough. She's slated to be in surgery for 2–3 hours. We ask for prayer for the surgeon's hands to be steady and able after a long day, the anesthesiologist to be brilliant, for Tebb to be without pain before, during, and after, and for everything to continue to go better than expected. Surgery begins at 11pm. The primary surgeon, we learn, is one of the preeminent wrist surgeons in the world (of course he is).

Surgery finishes at 1:30am. The waiting room is empty except for us. We rush to the door to the operating area when it opens, and we speak to the surgeons. The surgery was successful. Super surgeon uses his phone to show us pictures of Tebb's wrist before and after surgery. They removed the broken bone protruding from her wrist, filled the area with bone mortar (compound from corpses) and braced it with titanium rods on both sides. She will have full use of her wrist after an extended rehabilitation. She did great with the anesthesia. We shared:

"Surgery on wrist (compound fracture) successful."

Update from Paula: "Tebben's catheter is now out. Hallelujah ❤ Her pelvic fracture doesn't require surgery. Her facial fracture doesn't require surgery although the surgeon said he could fix the barely perceptible indent in her upper cheekbone. It'll be her call. She is resting well but still pretty out of it bc of the pain meds she needs to feel comfortable with her wrist. The neurosurgeon said she can travel as early as one week but that would be by transport to another hospital in the US - probably Houston. We're still figuring it out. Full restoration and healing will take between 4–6 months. THAT AINT NOTHIN!!! Praise JESUS ❤ Pls continue healing prayers for NO PAIN so drugs can be lessened, finger movement for circulation in wrist and hand, full consciousness and short term memory intact again. Thank u to all GODS ANGELS out there 💛 We couldn't do this without ur prayers."

"The Lord will fight for you; you need only be still." Exodus 14:14. This is the prophetic word over all of us now. So, the morning after surgery, Tebben has some pain in her wrist. We pray that Jesus takes it from her, and when I ask her, "Tiene dolor?" she answers, "un poco." Thank you Jesus. Thereafter, Tebben has a nice lunch of chicken broth, orange, and some Jell-O.

7/20/16 Social Media Updates:

"Tebben just moved the fingers on her right hand on her own! Philippians 4:13

Tebben just moved all of her fingers at the same time to try to make a fist! Fist of healing fury!"

"She just wiggled all of her fingers!"

"No matter how many promises God has made they are yes in Christ and so through Him the amen is spoken by us to the Glory of God." 2 Corinthians 1:20. As you have been reading about, God has kept all his promises to us and our family about his mercy and grace. Pray that today, He lift Tebben Gill Lopez out of the morphine cloud, and she is moved to a regular hospital room where they will allow the three of us to stay for the remainder of her hospital stay. Can I get an amen!"

Amen. To see movement that quickly after surgery inspires us and the formation of a fist symbolizes Tebb's fighting spirit. It also speaks to the fighting to come on different battlefields: each other, our fears, the world and the enemy.

7/21/16 Social Media Posts:

"As Tebb emerges into more focused awareness, there have been some battles with fear and confusion as a result of the powerful effects of the narcotics and her reality. Regardless, she has found strength in the name of Jesus, prayer and his word. Last night we prayed James 4: 7,8 and 1 John 4:4. Please read these verses out loud and pray them into Tebben today."

"Blessed is the king who comes in the name of the Lord! Peace in heaven and glory in the highest." Luke 19:38 We read this during

the morning reading and praised Him. Be in His Word and receive His strength."

From Paula:

"Today was another good day. Another day of firsts. For the first time since the accident Tebb: ate two solid food meals (albeit tiny bites, but slow and steady wins the race), had the longest periods of consciousness that she's had (attributed to no more morphine), used a bedpan, engaged with the physical therapist - moving her fingers on her right hand on command to stimulate the healing of her wrist (Daniel the PT was very pleased with the decreased inflammation in her fingers due to the fairly ongoing massaging that Ray and I did all day). Tebb's still groggy but not like she was. Every day is better and we are SO GRATEFUL TO GOD and the prayers of the saints (all of you). Praise Jesus ♥ Three highlights of my day: 1) An older weathered Limanan woman was sitting in the corner of our waiting room camp, her grandson was in an accident. She asked Tebb's friend Isabel why we were there. Isabel shared in Spanish. The woman replied that she couldn't sleep last night because of her grandson's accident so she prayed all night long. The wise woman said "God is SO good. He gives us evidence of his greatness and He doesn't leave us alone." I took that to mean that He pokes and prods us with His encouraging presence because that's what He's been doing since the second we found out about Tebb's accident. The next moment after Isabel translated the woman's words I got a text from my sister Carla with a link to a blog post. Contained in the post was this verse from Isaiah: "For I am the Lord your God who takes hold of your right hand and says to you, "Do not fear, I will help you." (Isaiah 41:13). Brought me to tears of joy. It's Tebb's right wrist that is broken and caused her excruciating pain at times. 2) I bought some fresh beet, pear, lemon, apple & ginger juice and Tebb indicated she wanted to have some. I asked the head nurse for permission to let her have some and she said yes. Tebb was giddy with excitement at the prospect of sipping some fresh juice. 3) Lunch today was a delight. It was just me and Tebb and we had an extended time of conscious conversation. She was smiling and understanding more and more. Pls continue to pray for clearance out of ICU into a regular room tomorrow, for a medical transport flight home to CT and against the negative effects of the anesthesia (she's was a little anxious tonight). We're meditating on Exodus 14:14 - *The Lord your God will fight for you, you need only be still.* 💙💙 *Thank you for all your love.*"

"Amazing Grace. So all understand how God is working here. I know you have all been keeping track of Tebben's progress. In answer to the prayers she is really waking up today, which creates more challenges for us all. Everyone knows she is a fighter and can be a little impatient at times. She is ready to go to the next step! Today, while her PT, John Eric Angeles, was working with her fingers, she was experiencing some significant pain and Tebb and I prayed that Jesus take her pain. This released John and he began to prophecy into her life, specifically Jeremiah 29:11, about the plans God has for prospering her. This is the same verse that Sheryl prayed over us on the plane from Newark to Orlando. John told Tebb that he and his wife are praying for her every day, and we prayed together before he left. "Aren't all angels ministering spirits sent to serve those who will inherit salvation." Hebrews 1:14. So all understand."

At this point we almost need to create a chart to document all the dots God is connecting for us.

From Paula:

"Today was another good day. 🙏 Entering the ICU I met Dr. Torres Marquez the neurologist who is the point dr. for Tebb's care. He was not entirely thrilled with her progress and said he needed her to eat more and use the bedpan (with assistance of course). I was not happy hearing he was not thrilled, as I was extremely thrilled with her progress. The doctor ordered MRIs to check her pelvis and head. When I arrived in Tebb's room around 9am she was awake and engaged for about 4 hours, fell sound asleep for about a 1/2 hour and I had to wake her up to eat lunch. I hated to do it but she wasn't going to be able to eat for 8 hours before her MRIs at 9pm so she had to eat at noon or not until 10pm. Tebb was up for the remainder of the day talking a blue streak and entertaining her friend, Laura, who arrived today from Ollanta. Laura works and lives with Tebb. Tebben was still a little frustrated bc she is not able to remember things especially in immediate short-term memory. But at one point in the late *afternoon a switch flipped when she with only Ray and I and though her short term memory is still elusive, she took an entirely different stance. In a metaphysical dissertation she shared that she was going to change from being a victim to whom things were happening to an empowered observer of her experience. Instead of focusing on what she can't do, she decided to focus on what she can do. Our mouths were agape in awe. So what she can do today that she couldn't yesterday:1) eat almost all her eggs for breakfast 2) eat a piece of buttered bread by herself with her left hand 3) engage more fully in PT by opening and closing her fingers on her right hand 4) use the bedpan 5) stay awake in conscious conversation all day 6) accept and be with her circumstances. Given the progress she made today the doctor gave permission to move out of ICU into her new room tonight after the MRIs but recommended she sleep one more night in ICU and move tomorrow. It was Tebben's call and she agreed. Hallelujah!!! God is SO GOOD ❣ Pls pray for good MRI reports so we can move to the next step in her healing. She's in having the MRI now. Tebben is "SO BORED." She wants to gets up and move around. Pls pray she can do that soon bc she's getting a little feisty - miraculously bordering on obnoxious. To God be ALL HONOR, PRAISE and GLORY. Thank u Lord Jesus for bringing us back our little girl. 🙏 ✝ ✝ 🖤🖤 Therefore I tell you whatever you ask for in pray, believe that you have received it, and it will be yours. -Mark 11:24 💚💚*

"So, Paula is halfway through drafting the next update (it's been a great day), but I must share that we spent the greater part of the afternoon listening as Tebben orated her doctoral dissertation on meta-physics and the collective unconscious as they connect to interpersonal relationships and mindfulness. It was quite a bit beyond my intellect but I did absorb parts of it. I'm not kidding. I wish I recorded it."

The 21st is a miraculous day. To see Tebben being healed by her own faith is a blessing. To see her mind working at such a high level in spite of her TBI is powerful. She built a bridge between the physical and metaphysical, crossed that spiritual bridge into her future and saw the healing of her mind and body! God's continuing faithfulness is evident in Tebb's physical therapist, John

Angeles, who brought us back to where we began our journey when he prayed Jeremiah 29:11 into Tebb's life, while healing her wounded hand: "For I know the plans I have for you declares the Lord . . . "

7/22/16 Posts:

"Another prophetic word of God, this one a word of wisdom through Tebben Gill Lopez. The other night she was telling Paula and I about how she helped Jesus care for the unborn babies. Her prophetic PT, John Eric Angeles, who prayed a prophetic word through Jeremiah 29:11 into her life and His plans to prosper her, told me this morning that his ✦♥⚱✦♥🤍💙 wife, Catherine, is pregnant with their first child, Nathan, who will become a missionary. At that moment, God made it clear that Tebben was praying for Nathan, their unborn baby. This is Holy Spirit/prophetic PT. We end each session in prayer. We prayed for God's plans for Tebben and Nathan. "

"This is the cleanest hospital I have ever been in. There are people cleaning every nook and cranny-24/7. I think they might be cyborgs. I'll check with Tebben Gill Lopez. She would most certainly know if this is the case and where they fall on the time warp continuum."

"Tebben left the ICU today and the 3 of us are now sharing a private room together in the hospital. Thank you Jesus."

Things are happening fast. The supernatural becomes natural in the space between us, where we connect through faith and the Holy Spirit.

7/23/16 Posts

From Paula:

"Elaborating on Ray's update-TODAY WAS ANOTHER GOOD DAY. The room is way larger than our hotel room was, smells way better, friends can hang out with her, we're no longer paying for a hotel BUT MORE IMPORTANTLY we get to be with Tebb through the night to calm some of her residual anxiety from meds and trauma. PRAISE JESUS ❤ Peace I leave with you; my peace I give you. I do not give to you as the world gives. Do not let your hearts be troubled and do not be afraid.

-John 14:27

Tebben has been walking to the bathroom (a few feet from her bed) , con ayuda de sus padres, and she just took a shower! More to come. Philippians 4:13"

7/24/16 "She's back with us again. Amen. Thank you for the prayers. The IV is out-no more antibiotics. One more positive step forward. Tebben has been suffering throughout the night and into this morning with delirium and paranoia, a side effect of the morphine that swam through her body when she was sedated. Please pray for her healing and deliverance.

"For God did not give us a spirit of timidity but a spirit of love, power and

self discipline." 2 Timothy 1:7

Tebb is obsessed with three things: eating, going to the bathroom, and messing with her IV. She wants to go to the bathroom every five minutes and tells us it will only take "a hot second." I have never heard this expression before but I'm beginning to understand what it means. It's dangerous for her to get up, which is why she has a bedpan that we help her to use. But in the next few minutes she wants to go the bathroom "please for a hot second." We tell her no; use the bedpan. A few minutes after breakfast she asks when we're going to have lunch and keeps asking every five or ten minutes. She keeps pulling at the bandages around the IV in her right wrist and late one night she eventually rips it out with her teeth when Paula dozed off for a second. Fortunately, it was coming out that day anyway, and we are all very much relieved about that. It's one less thing.

The attacks come at night. Tebb wants to get up and use the bathroom "please just for a hot second." We are exhausted and trying to get some sleep. It's a small room with a recliner and a very hard couch. Paula gets in bed with Tebb but needs help because Tebb is delirious. She doesn't recognize us. "Who are you People? What are you doing to me? Why are you in my bed?" We have her trapped between us. I am at the bottom of the bed and Paula at the top. We are using our legs and arms to stop Tebb from jumping out of bed and hurting herself. She is strong and fights us. She bites my arm! As dawn creeps in through the crack at the bottom of the shades, we are exhausted from wrestling with the enemy all night, but we are safe, unharmed, and we have peace; we have victory.

7/25/16 Posts

"Another difficult night but better than last night- no night terrors/confusion only anger and frustration. Paula is very tired. We are going to try to walk with Tebben a bit today. Yesterday Tebb had a wonderful time with her friends-much laughter. The physical healing is powerful and wonderful to behold. Tebben needs to regain her strength and energy. We are at a point where we will be focusing more directly on getting home. An update in the prophetic spiritual realm to follow. Three thousand words- down the hall and back-Tebben is bad ass!

Our Victory Walk in Jesus!

I mentioned how blessed we are by Tebb's prophetic PT, John Angeles. When Tebben was sedated in ICU last week, John told me that he and his wife are expecting their first child, Nathan, who has been in his mother's womb for 7 months. He said they are praying that he become a missionary. Today after PT, Tebben prayed for John in Espanol and prayed for the protection of their son who will be a great missionary. A word of wisdom to bless John and his wife Catherine. "Follow the way of love and eagerly desire gifts of the Spirit, especially prophecy." 1 Corinthians 14:1"

7/26/16 Post

"So. The hospital has been in touch with Blue Cross/Blue Shield and here is the Mexican Standoff/Catch 22- Although Tebben would qualify for medical evacuation at this time due to her physical and mental health conditions (Post Traumatic Delirium) it is not covered by our policy unless she needs treatment that can't be provided by the hospital. Such medical transport would costs 100s of thousands of dollars I'm sure. The hospital is trying to work with the insurance company to explore coverage for medical evacuation but it's a chess match balancing between the insurance business and the ethics/honest integrity of the medical providers. Please pray for God to connect the dots for all the players to result in immediate medical transport to the States that is fully covered by Blue Cross/BlueShield."

7/27/16

"Oh! And I forgot to mention an awesome visit from Louisa! And let me thank God for the army of Ollanta Ex-Pats, ministering Angels, who have helped us in immeasurable ways: Jason Grover, Vivian Smith Baca, Michelle Gatt, Juan Mayorga, his father, "Lolo," Rosanna Giorlandino, aka "Rosa," Isabel Eskin Shapson, Laura Brokaw and the prayers of all those in the Ollanta family. We love you forever. Another tough night for Tebben. Paula and I had to literally sit in bed with her until 3:30 am to prevent her from tearing off her soft caste and going to the bathroom continuously every 5 minutes. This is with 1.5 mg of Klonipin, which is not working. However, she seemed less fearful and angry.

Some of my observations from Peru: all the women are beautiful and less than .05 percent of the population smokes. ALSO, TEBBEN'S WOLVERINE HEALING CONTINUES. TOMORROW SHE GETS THE STITCHES REMOVED FROM HER ARM. WHAT? THAT'S RIGHT. YOU HEARD ME CORRECTLY. SHE HAS BEEN ABLE TO PUT PRESSURE ON HER RIGHT WRIST FOR A FEW

*DAYS. WE'VE BEEN STRESSING ABOUT IT BUT THE OR-
THOPEDIC SURGEON SAID IT WAS FINE. AND REMEMBER
THE BROKEN RIBS? IF ANYONE HAS SUFFERED THE SAME
SAY AMEN IF YOU RECALL THE PAIN FELT WITH EVERY
BREATH. NOT A MENTION OF PAIN FROM TEBBEN. I BET
IF WE TOOK ANOTHER X-RAY WE WOULD FIND NOTHING.
ANOTHER GOOD DAY AFTER A LONG NIGHT'S JOURNEY.
ANOTHER 200 FOOT WALK DOWN THE HALLWAY, WALKS
AROUND OTHER PARTS OF THE CLINICA AND A WHEEL-
CHAIR RIDE OUTSIDE INTO THE COURTYARD TO CELE-
BRATE THE FIRST TIME WE'VE SEEN THE SUN SINCE WE'VE
BEEN HERE. IT'S 7:00 PM IN LIMA AND WE WILL BE EXPE-
RIENCING NEW MEDICATION TONIGHT. PLEASE PRAY FOR
US. ALSO, THANKS TO THE LOVE AND SUPPORT OF FAMILY,
PLANS FOR OUR RETURN TO CT ARE WELL UNDERWAY! Did
I just write the majority of this update in CAPS? As if the words are
not powerful enough on their own. How annoying?"*

7/28/16 Post

*"The Lord will fight for you; you need only be still." Exodus
14:14 How do we receive this? Stop it. Whatever you are doing and/
thinking and just breath-recite the verse again and again in your
mind, in your heart meditate, make it your mantra. There are many
but this verse has been the lifesaver in the middle of the vast stormy
sea. A quick update on Paula and myself. She has been Tebben's lifesaver and I am in awe of the endless depth of her love and courage.
My back is like one twisted spasmodic muscle and I have a full beard
for the first time. God spoke to me on the morning Starbucks run. (I
saw graffiti, "Trust God Even When His Answer is Wait") on a wall
near achurch on the rotary. It was written in English. We are under
heavy attack right now in terms of Tebb's mental health almost a
perpetual state of anxiety/frustration- and she is also very week from
the night terrors she experienced and the Klonopin we had to give.
We are working with the doctors on finding meds that will work for
her anxiety. Keep praying hard. Today started out a little rough but
ended up being the best day, as Tebben came fully back to us for a
few hours this afternoon. She was engaged in deep, rational thought*

and even saw that I was stressed and asked me if I was OK and if there was anything she could do for me. We also discussed with her our situation here and how it impacts on us and the rest of the family with respect to our plans to come home. She expressed compassion and concern for both Paula and myself and prayed a sweet prayer of healing and wisdom for us all. She spoke to her brother Jesse today and was thrilled! She also spoke to her Uncle Jon and her Cousin Hannah. Likewise, she couldn't of been happier. Later, she cried tears of joy when she found out that her cousin Meredith is getting married, we will all be there and she is a bride's maid. Her short term memory is still absent but her long term is good."

The story behind this is one of pride and machismo. Klonopin has been a nightmare. It turns Tebben into Regan from *The Exorcist*. Paula has researched anti-psychotic meds and has spoken to her sister, Carla's high school friend, Darren, who is a neurologist at Yale for the VA. Gathering and reviewing all the data, she finds a med we want to try. We're having a consult with Dr. Torres, stand-in for Dr. Hinojosa who's on vacation, through an interpreter, and when he understands that we're questioning the use of Klonopin, he becomes angry. How dare we question his expertise and judgment! Finally, after some very tense uncomfortable minutes, his resident calms him down and he agrees to bring in a doctor from the psychiatric department for a consult. The psychiatrist is another angel. Her name is Carla Cortez. Carla agrees with Paula and Darren and prescribes Seroquel. She has a two-year old. Carla gives Paula her home number and tells her to call with any questions.

My mind explodes. It's been two weeks since Tebb's accident; she's been awake since July 17, and they haven't had her evaluated by a psychiatrist! Blue Cross/Blue Shield has already told me that Tebb would qualify for Medical Repatriation, but it is not covered under my basic policy. They also advise that exceptions can be made under extraordinary circumstances when the patient is not receiving adequate care. This missing piece is extraordinary, and BC/BS eventually agrees. This is another answer to prayer. God has provided a way. The catch is the lead physician also has to agree.

7/29/16 Posts

"Great night of mostly restful sleep for Tebben after an amazing afternoon/ evening the day before and a great morning so far, as we put together the final pieces for our return trip and I set a lifetime PR with 85 push-ups on my first set this morning. So, the plot takes another turn. I just got off the phone with another nurse from BC/ BS, and he advised that although it is not covered under our policy, Dr. Subeh's recommendation is air ambulance repatriation with a medical nurse. This will be discussed further, Doctor to Doctor between Subeh and Hinijosa this afternoon. This recommendation of course will have to be approved by the bullshit department but this is a complete 180

from the original medical recommendation.

It's been a great day for Tebb. We sang a medley of rock songs together, took over the entire clinic by walking and rocking the wheelchair, laughed and Paula and me cut through a lot of the bullshit. I've been in touch with Laura Lynne from Gaylord Rehab in Wallingford, CT and BC/BS (bull crap/ bullshit) medical staff. The doctor to doctor conversation is hopefully happening as write this post and all medical records will be emailed by tomorrow morning. PRAY WE HAVE ANOTHER GOOD NIGHT. Catching some rays outside Starbucks in Lima. I don't see anybody else sitting around here bare chested. Some other observations from Lima-8:00 am really means 8:30–9:00; there is a layer of dust over everything, but thisproblem is more prevalent in the mountain regions, such as Ollanta; pigeons rule in Lima-they are deadly to other birds.

It's always such a blessing when God answers our prayers in such a timely way. BC/BS is ready to pay for the repatriation. Hinijosa just has to sign off. They do it all the time, or so I've been told. I know I have been a bear during this time. I look the part with my beard hanging down about six inches from my chin. All the men in Lima are meticulously groomed. I have fought to gather the records. They must come through the lead physician, which is Hinijosa or his partner, Dr. Torres. They are difficult to get a hold of. Torres has been angry and prideful. I learn that he has been angry since his young daughter died ten years ago. I pray for his peace. I go back and forth with BC/BS, but God is always in control. I'm on the phone with Dr. Subeh when Hinijosa walks onto the floor. I approach him. Our limited abilities in Spanish and English are enough for me to explain the circumstances, and I hand him my phone. All he has to do is agree with Subeh and off we go. He doesn't but it doesn't matter. We surrender.

7/30/16 Posts

"Tebben read all the messages today. A great night for Tebb. She woke up at 11:30 and 2:30 to use the bathroom and went back to bed without a whimper. Our repatriation medical escort flight lands at JFK at 22:00 on Monday, 8/1 and we should be home in Shelton after midnight."

7/31/16 Posts

"A few more observations about Lima. Classic cars are rare-mostly newer Hondas, Nissans, Kias, Hyundai's, etc...the same as in the US; people aren't sure what side of the sidewalk they want to walk on; family is everything there is much love here- God is every-where-God is love- 1 Corinthians 13:8- look it up and read it! Esto Es esto. Good restful night for Tebb and we all slept in until around 8. Homeward Bound in motion. Tebb is really focused on her desire to get home, which makes her sad because it can't happen sooner. Pray for peace for us all. Also in motion is the Peru push-up movement. Ordinarily, today is my Sabbath but based on the number of people I hear from who are now doing push-ups, which is certainly secondary to those who are praying and reading their Bibles like never before, God freed me to work out today and I set a new PR with 95 push-ups on my first set. So, to join in the movement and receive His strength, join me at 5:00 am today (4:00 am for those on EST) to crank out 3 sets of maximum reps per set. I will be leaving 100 on the ground in Lima on my 1st set. Read Philippians 4:13 and 2 Corinthians 12:9."

I did 100 pushups!

8/1/16 Post

"Tebben, Paula & Ray safely on 2nd flight. Departed San Salvador a few minutes ago and scheduled to arrive in JFK ~10PM. AV570. -p"

8/2/16 Post

"We're home."

I never return to the office and am officially retired from federal law enforcement on August 31, 2016. I am Tebb's physical therapist, and we work together every morning. I am a slave driver, and she is a Spartan—a perfect match. At this point she has no memory of the accident, which is a blessing and scary at the same time. Her pre-accident memories of Peru are very cloudy, but if I show her a photograph she can tell me where it was taken and who is in the photo. The images trigger her memories of the stories that go with the pictures. She still doesn't know what happened. She knows she was in a bad accident in Peru and lives with her injuries daily. But she hasn't asked for details yet, and I'm praying for the right moment and words to explain. We've been home about two weeks when I receive an epiphany from the Lord on how to explain to Tebb what happened to her: "Hey Tebb." "Yeah." "You know how people say, 'at least you didn't get hit by a bus,' to put things in perspective by saying that whatever it is they're dealing with it's not the worst thing that could've happened?" "Yeah." (her tone is now hesitant and suspicious). "Well . . . you got hit by a bus." And that's how she found out, and so it goes.

Chapter 17

Second Death

AROUND NOON ON JULY 7, 2018, my sister Teresa and my nephew Jackson are driving to Dad's. Jackson is driving as he just got his permit. They visit Dad every day at around the same time. When they arrive, they find the cleaning lady inside already at work. Jackson walks in and goes straight to Dad's office because he's always in there working. Teresa comes in through the garage and sees Dad's Jeep is there. She and Jackson meet in the dining room and talk to the cleaning lady who says she hasn't seen him the whole time she's been in the house. She didn't see his car so she assumed he was gone. As they're talking in the dining room, Jackson looks down the basement stairs and sees Dad lying on the floor. He yells to Teresa, and they all run down the stairs. He's lying on his right side next to his stationary bike. Teresa tells Jackson to check his pulse while she and the cleaning lady turn him onto his back, and Teresa starts chest compressions. Jackson runs upstairs to get better reception and calls 911. He makes the call, gives them all the information he can and moves the car out of the driveway so they have easy access. He hears his mom crying out, "Please don't take him now, not yet!"

Teresa tells Jackson to call his uncles, and I'm the first one he calls. By this time, the basement is crowded with members of the Commack Volunteer Ambulance Corp trying their best, but Jackson knows his Grandpa is already with Grandma in heaven.

When everyone clears out of the basement, Jackson lays down next to his hero, his idol.

When I got the call, I told Jackson to be with his mother, and I called my younger brothers, Steve and Peter, while driving south on the Merritt Parkway. The entire drive I pray: "Please Lord, not now. Don't take him now." When I arrive around 2:00 pm, I go to the basement and find Jackson lying next to Dad, face to face, with his arm across Dad's chest.

The forensics are clear. Dad lifted weights for 20 minutes every day and rode his bike after lifting. He wore an Apple Watch with a fit app which shows that he was riding at a five-minute per mile rate. He rode three miles and was two minutes into the fourth mile when he stopped. There is a bloody scratch on his left ankle which shows that he got off the bike himself when he rode into crisis. The bike has locked-in pedals, so he had to have snapped out of them and scratched his left ankle in the process. There are no other wounds or bruises. Dad got off his bike for the last time and lay down alongside it facing the front wheel. His watch has a 911 feature that when activated would place a 911 call and alert all his contacts that the call was placed. We all like to believe that he intentionally didn't hit that button because he was tired and ready to be with his wife for the rest of eternity.

The following Saturday we have Dad's memorial service at Brugermann's Funeral Home, the same place where we had Mom's service. God has prepared me for this spiritually, mentally, and physically. It's been two years since Tebb's accident in Peru. She is strong, a daily miracle of healing, back to work and looking to buy a home near the beach. My mitigation work is growing, and physically, pound for pound, I've never been stronger in my life. I'm training for a meet in Vermont in August and deadlifted 655 lbs. in preparation for the competition. The Lord has blessed my training, knowing the physical strength he gives me pours into my mental and spiritual health and healing.

I am the head of the family. I need to lead. I need to be strong. I facilitate the service, like I did for Mom, and eulogize Dad, like I did for Mom. The room is full of people, family, friends, and some of Dad's former colleagues. My siblings are also ready to speak words of love, remembrances, and promise. This is the Eulogy God gave me:

"So many stories, moments, accomplishments but the most significant and wonderful aspect of his life was his relationship with our Mom. They knew each other as children growing up in the same neighborhood in Washington Heights. Dad was Mom's piano teacher. They experienced a colorful and eventful childhood and adolescence. Many of you have heard the stories, but I don't know how many know that they were both gang members. Dad was a member of The Vampires, and Mom was part of The Aqua Chicks. They were innocent social clubs. The Vampires had a tackle football team, and I don't know what the Aqua Chicks did but I suspect it had something to do with water. As I understand it, Mom was originally interested in Uncle Ramon, and they dated at least once, but shortly thereafter the romance between my parents began. They married after Dad returned from Manila where he served in the Air Force during the Korean War. He was an auto mechanic but was recruited by the band because he could play the flute. As Dad would tell you, he could play several instruments: the piano, guitar, flute to name a few. He was a musical jack-of-all-trades but the master of none. He also reported that although military life as a member of the band could be viewed as light duty, there was the ever-present threat of the indigenous Hucks, who would execute ambushes on American troops coming down from the hills armed with machetes. I believe this was an actual threat, but fortunately, not toward the base where our Dad served. They were married on December 27, 1953. I'm not sure when they moved into that cold water flat at 268 Wilson Avenue in the Bushwick Section of Brooklyn, but Teresa was born in June '58; I came along in September '59, and one month later we moved to 4 Sarina Drive in Commack. Steve showed up in '62 and Pete popped out in '64 to complete the clan.

Early Life Lessons: My earliest memories of Dad are of him giving us horseback rides and his hard work ethic and academic pursuits. He would come home from a long day's work at Wheeler Labs in Smithtown and go off to class at Manhattan College, where he was studying for his master's degree in Electrical Engineering. When things became more settled later in life, Dad was a Little League coach for me and my brothers and was revered, perhaps not by all the parents, for making sure that every player on the team got equal playing time. This often took precedence over winning. His involvement with us in sports was also a lifelong pursuit. He participated in many triathlons with Steve and Pete and also trained and competed with me in powerlifting in the mid-to-late '90s. His best competition bench was 219 lbs.

Dad always took the time to speak words of wisdom to us. He constantly emphasized the importance of being a balanced person by developing your:

Mind, body and personality/or character: This was his own lifelong pursuit. His intelligence/mathematics and electronics are legendary. I'm not smart enough to understand it all but he was a giant in the field of electronic engineering specializing in antenna design and first microwave, then later GPS landing systems for jet aircraft. He published numerous articles and is referenced in others, including technical textbooks. I've heard of references to "The Lopez Feed." Academically, he was ABD (all but dissertation towards his Ph.D.) and he reveled in taking on the academics. He has over 50 patents, numerous awards and is an IEEE fellow, the highest honor in electronic engineering. However, perhaps one of his greatest technical achievements was when he beat a speeding ticket by going to court and explaining the margin of error on a radar gun.

The development of his mind continued till the day he died. He devoted time every day to his studies, problem solving and mind expansion. In the last few years, he spent time playing chess against the computer and was always ready to respond to questions from young engineers in the field. His devotion to exercise and competition was essential/foundational to my growth and development. When he was 18, he came in 9th in the New York State Road Race, which qualified him to go to Utah for a chance to make the U.S. Olympic Team, but Pop had suffered a stroke at the time and he stayed home to support Tita and the family. He was constantly on the bike, on the road in spring and summer and the rollers in his workshop in the study during the winter. He road just about every day of the year, had hundreds of trophies he donated to local trophy shops. During our childhood, we attended many road races in Central Park and at a track somewhere in one of the five boroughs. He was the one Hispanic on the German Bicycle Sports Club. The day he went to be with the Lord, he lifted weights and had ridden for approximately 15 minutes on his bike in the basement when he got off and went off to be with Mom.

Later in life, Dad's philosophy evolved to add a fourth component, "Love," that being for family, friends and mankind in general. Everyone who's met Dad would agree that he was one of the nicest people.

Other Words of Wisdom: "If you don't have problems you're not living." "When you're up, don't be too up because you're always going to have your downs and when your down, don't get too down because you're always going to have your ups."

Spiritual Journey: My paternal grandparents were devout Roman Catholics and raised my Dad and Uncles accordingly. They loved God and had great faith. As such, we were also raised Roman Catholic. We all might agree that Dad was one of the smartest people any of us have known. And, his intelligence challenged his faith. So, he was an agnostic throughout his adult life. Mom's stroke in 2003 and death in 2010 took Dad on a spiritual journey, which eventually brought him back to his parents' faith. As many of you may know, I became a Christian at the age of 19 and can be quite outspoken about my faith at times. My Dad certainly heard it from me often and at one point told me he had heard enough. One of my most cherished memories of Dad is a few years after Mom passed. We were at my brother-in-law, Jon Gill's, surprise 50th birthday party and Dad and I were talking. He said to me, "You know Ray I been praying and giving it a lot of thought and for me it's Christ, what my parents taught me, but I'm not going around telling people what to believe in or what to do." I said, "That's good Dad. It's all good Dad."

Towards the end of Mom's life I spent a lot of time as one of her caretakers on the weekends and would always pray for her and Dad before I left. He always received (or tolerated) it. One day, before I *was about to leave, He said to me, "You know Ray I also pray to God and lately I've been praying that he takes your mother home." I said, "That's good Dad." Mom passed about two weeks later.*

My Dad taught me a lot about strength and power and I am blessed to have shared some of his words of love and wisdom with you today. I take it all in with what I've learned from him and my God in whom I trust and lean on in pursuit of those ideals

"For God did not give us a spirit of timidity, but a spirit of love, power and self-discipline." 1 Timothy 2:7

"I can do all things through Christ." Philippians 4:13

We thought he'd live to 100, like his mother but that changed, in a moment last Saturday. James 4:14 states "You do not even know what will happen tomorrow. What is your life? You are a mist that appears for a little while then vanishes." This is how Dad lived. He showed us the way. This is why we have to live each day loving each other with our words and deeds.

The only time I saw my father cry was when we placed our mother's ashes at the cemetery. Well, there are no tears in Heaven. Hebrews 11:1 says, "For faith is the substance of things hoped for, the evidence of things unseen." We can't see them but we believe they are together and he's playing the piano and singing their song to Mom, You Light up My Life. It was a very special song for them. It helped them to get through the good times and some bad times."

Teresa's sketch of Dad

Chapter 18

The Winter of My Depression

GOD'S BLESSINGS CONTINUE TO pour down. In 2011, I started training at Hard Kore, a powerlifting/strongman gym in Shelton owned by Lou Santella and his wife, Rose. I hadn't competed in over two years, still coming back from the torn hamstring I sustained at Southside Barbell in 2008. That was brutal. Beyond a mere pulled hamstring, when you tear part of the largest muscle in the body, it takes a tremendous amount of force and feels like you've been hit with a 16-lb sledgehammer. The larger the muscle, the more blood cells so the internal bleeding is quite extensive. I had deep purple and blue bruising from the top of my right hamstring all the way down to the bottom of my foot. I tore it doing sumo deadlifts, trying to inspire an Iraq war vet who wanted to get into powerlifting despite having the top part of his right quadriceps blown away by an IED. I was training sumo to increase my conventional pull and was getting close to ten reps with 500 lbs. The problem that day was that I had shoveled the driveway covered with eight inches of wet snow the day before. The first rep felt heavy, and I should've stopped before I hit the sixth and final rep that ripped the muscle apart. I guess I was showing off, just a little. It gave me another testimony of God's great healing power as the muscle reattaches itself over time. Then you need to do that deep muscle massage to break up the scar tissue and loosen up the fascia.

I met my training partner, Lenny Creatura, at Hard Kore. He is a freak of nature. He's 63, as I write this, and doesn't look a day over 45, in part because he shaves his head. He's 5'6" and weighs a solid 215 lbs. of massive muscle. He's a lifetime drug-free lifter, and his training methods make young men puke.

I did my comeback meet, The Police/Fire World Championships, in September 2011 at the Javits Center in New York City. There were 15,000 athletes from over 30 different countries. There was one lifter from the Mongolian Police. It was a big meet and good to be back. My dad, John Wood, and Brother Jerry all came out to support me that day.

Hard Kore Fitness fit right in with the prophetic word over my life, as there were plenty of hardcore lifters and numerous opportunities for ministry and prayer. The gym closed down about a year before Dad passed, and we ended up going to Hellbent Barbell in Stratford, which is a reemergence of sorts from the old Southside Barbell, started by Rob Tonini and Frank Gomes with a lot of the old South Side Gym equipment. Still moving into the prophetic word, powerlifting is perfect because it can easily become self-idolatry, worshipping your own body and strength, some willing to take performance enhancing drugs and risk injury to get stronger. I've never used drugs, but I have certainly risked and sustained injuries including a stress fracture in the L4/SI vertebrae, two biceps tears, a bone spur removed from my right triceps and my torn hamstring. Physical power is addictive, and I have been filled with boastful pride. Those are the times that God will take you down. But he was building me up before and after Dad's passing. Lenny, myself, Len's son, Tony, and a bunch of other lifters from Hellbent went up to Vermont in August 2018 to compete. I have been competing deadlift only since 2012 because I'm bone on bone in my shoulders. When I go to a full meet, since the deadlift is the last event, I have all day to relax and help my teammates prepare.

I'm working with Lenny during his warm-ups when he gets severe cramps and muscle spasms in his lower back. He's in agony, and he can't move; he's thinking about pulling out of the meet so he doesn't get hurt. Now I've prayed for Lenny before, and I know he's receptive. He's a solid Catholic Christian (you know who you are), and I offer to pray for his healing. I tell him I'm going to lay my hand over his lower back when I pray and not to worry about it. I pray and God does the work. He heals Len's back, and he not only competes but sets an all-time world records in the squat with a 550 lb. raw lift and with his 1,520 lb. total! I ended up deadlifting 655 lbs. in the 181-lb master division.

My 655-lb. pull in Maine in August 2018

There's a lot of old man strength on show that day and all the young dudes are watching. We're very excited and a couple of weeks later, back in the gym, I hear Len talking about the meet. When I hear him say that "Ray prayed and healed me," I'm quick to interrupt and share that God did the healing through Len's faith!

It's all good. Paula and I had prayed that God give me two to three death penalty cases a year. He had other plans, and I'm getting several a year. I'm believing that I can deadlift 700 soon.

God's blessing our marriage and the kids are alright. Then there's a crash landing.

There are no good reasons for my descent into that dark self-loathing pit. It's just the opposite; I have everything to rejoice about. Yes. Mom and Dad are gone but reunited in heaven. It makes no sense, but each day it gets harder to get out of bed. As the days drag on, I can only look forward to going to sleep. I'm functioning; going to the gym but not getting stronger, meeting my clients, chasing records, talking with lawyers, even going to conferences, but I'm anxious all the time; I'm the walking dead. I white knuckle it, tough it out. I rationalize and self-diagnose, telling my family and friends that I've had a delayed reaction to the loss of my father, that I'm just in a funk. When you lose one parent the universe shakes, but when both parents are gone the universe is forever altered.

I'm not sleeping well. I go to bed exhausted but fearful that I'll wake up and not be able to get back to sleep. I do my breathing meditation on the name of Jesus, or his word, " . . . be still . . . " but it just gets darker, and I start thinking about killing myself, about how I might do it; I've got my .357 magnum; I've got my vehicle. And I'm lying to everyone, telling them I'm okay.

Jesse's living in Long Island and Tebb's in her own home. But Paula can see and feel what's happening to me. I fight the enemy! These are the days of my flesh but like Jesus I offer up " . . . prayers and supplications with loud cries and tears . . . " Hebrews 5:7.

Paula is incredibly busy in her life. Her mother was just placed in assisted living in Shelton, and in addition to her academic responsibilities, Paula is consumed with helping her mother adjust. This battle couldn't have come at a worse time. But she fights for me and calls out the enemy in the name of Jesus. I'm 59 years old. The last time I fought this battle was 30 years ago. There's no sense to it. It's just the enemy trying to kill me, again. I'm past the suicidal ideation. I know my love for the Lord, my wife, and family is too strong, but I'm also ready to go home.

I make an appointment with my primary doctor. He's glad I came to see him. On December 4, 2018, I go to see a psychiatrist.

I'm diagnosed with Clinical Depression and started on Wellbutrin. He explains the neurochemistry, the synapses, and neurotransmitters. He tells me his patients all talk about returning to their normal selves. I know mental illness is now part of the health discussion. It has taken its place alongside addiction and other diseases.

I know it's been less than two weeks, but I don't feel any different. That morning of victory on December 17, I've been lying in bed for hours. I can't get up. I can't speak. All I can do is moan and groan. Paula's there; she's beside me, she's yelling at the devil. She tells me that I have to get up or she's taking me to the emergency room, and I know it's time to move. So I get up and go to the gym.

Lenny's there as usual. He's always there. He's been watching me and has seen me changing, looking weaker and more tired. We talk enough and he knows enough to know. I've also lied to him, saying once I get out of bed I'm fine. That's a lie. But on this day God answers our prayers; he restores my strength. I pull 585 lbs. sumo, and he releases the endorphins to give me that Holy Spirit jump-start I need! He reminds me that I need to join in my own healing and tells me again to "... strengthen your feeble arms and weak knees; make level paths for your feet so that the lame shall no longer be disabled but rather healed." Hebrews 12:12

My 585-lb. pull on December 17

And the struggle continues. I don't judge others but I'm Ray Lopez, so why am I on meds? My faith must not be strong enough, my prayers not powerful enough. I fall back and let the devil get in more strikes.

I'm reading Romans one day and God reminds me in 8:28 that " . . . in all things God works for the good of those who love him, who have been called according to his purpose." I'm not 19 in a psych hospital, and this isn't Lithium and Thorazine. Over time the right combination of Wellbutrin and Effexor brings me peace. My Christian pride will not get in the way of God's plans for the post-season of my life. And so it goes.

"He gives strength to the weary and increases the power of the weak. Even youths grow tired and weary and young men stumble and fall; but those who hope in the Lord will renew their strength. They will fly on wings like eagles; they will run and not grow weary; they will walk and not be faint." Isaiah 40: 29–31

Chapter 19

The Wind Cries Mary

I COULD NEVER FULLY describe the power of God, the love when a soul leaves the body for Heaven. But my sister-in-law's story reveals the start of the feeling, sharing His presence on holy ground.

Steve and Mary went on their first date on October 15, 2008. They met through Match.com. They were both divorcees with adult children. Steve was living in an apartment in Stow, Ohio. Mary was renting a home with an option to buy in Cuyahoga Falls, Ohio, where she ran a successful daycare business. She had her associate degree in Early Childhood Education and was excellent with kids. She loved children. She loved *Mary Poppins* and *Winnie the Pooh* and sought to bring the magic of God into her kids' lives through the love of Christ and the power of the Holy Spirit. Mary was a woman of powerful faith emerging from a broken home and difficult divorce. Steve had divorced in 2006 after 24 years of marriage with his first wife, Bobbie. They were both searching for each other.

They met at a coffee shop in Stow. Steve arrived early. When Mary walked in he saw a person who appeared somewhat timid. During this first date he took her all in and saw a beautiful woman, with short blonde hair, blue eyes, along with the presence of self-confidence and strength from within. Mary felt that Steve was looking directly into her soul.

Their romance progressed rapidly through a healing of two hearts. The Economic Recession of 2008/2009 brought them closer together. Mary lost her business, her home, and her car. Steve had reclaimed the home in Hudson, Ohio, where he and Bobbie raised their four children, and was living with his youngest son, Nicholas, who was still in high school. In January 2010 Mary moved in and they became a family.

The next few years were filled with golden days of God's glory. Mary's strong faith led Steve to Christ, and they became active in a local church. Steve and Mary started running together. Steve had been an avid runner and cyclist his entire life, and through exercising together, Mary received a healing of her mind, body, and spirit. She and Nicholas became very close. Mary found employment as a private nanny, trained hard, and she and Steve continued to fall deeply in love. After running the Women's Half Marathon at Disney World's Epcot Center in Florida, Steve proposed that evening during the fireworks display. Steve had always been a romantic.

On Valentine's Day of 2013, Steve was woken from his nap on the couch by Mya, a two-month-old puppy Mary gently placed on his stomach. She was a rescued Black Labrador/Pit Bull mix. Mary's daughter, Paige, had gone to a local animal shelter and found two pups that she liked. She kept one and told her mom about Mya. Mary loved her "Mya Mya," and at times Steve felt a little jealous.

Mary and Steve were married at their home in Hudson on October 5, 2013. Paula and I were blessed to sing one of Mary's Favorite songs for them, *That's What Faith Can Do* by Kutless. Steve's oldest son, Christopher, accompanied us on the guitar. Mary loved this song not for just the melody but the lyrics which framed her life of faith: " . . . *I've seen miracles just happen/Silent prayers get answered/Broken hearts become brand new/That's what faith can do . . .* "

Steve sold the Hudson house in March 2015, and they moved into their new home in University Heights, Ohio. Steve called it "The Outpost" because it was a temporary place to live, as he promised to buy Mary her dream home in a few years that included a wrap-around porch. But it was their first house together, and Mary rejoiced in making it into a home. She decorated and loved Steve and Nick through her homestyle cooking.

In October 2015, Steve took Mary to Paris to celebrate their anniversary. It was there that he first noticed the symptoms of ALS. Mary was having difficulties speaking which caused her to be more quiet than usual. Steve thought it was just fatigue or possibly allergies.

In November Mary went to visit her two best childhood friends, Vickie Huffman and Jenny DeRan. They were still living near her hometown of Fremont, Ohio. After Mary returned, Vickie contacted Steve via social media to ask if anything was going on with Mary, as she didn't appear to be her normal self. And so began their long journey.

That same month, Mary lost her job as a private nanny because the couple was concerned about her inability to communicate. She was devastated. Steve found out during a phone call with Mary while he was flying back from San Francisco on a Friday evening traveling for work. Hearing her tears on the phone with no way to hold and console her ripped at his heart.

Mary and Steve drove to Commack for Thanksgiving that year, and Paula and I prayed for her healing. I could see that she was scared, but also felt the force of her faith and knew her trust in the Lord and her hope for a complete healing. ALS is amongst the toughest of diseases. When I researched it online, I found only one story of a complete healing.

Mary's primary care physician first diagnosed her condition as reflux and then, suspecting allergies, sent her to an ENT (ear, nose, and throat) specialist. In January 2016, Steve noticed she was starting to have problems with hand strength. He did some research and asked her to see a neurologist. Steve's research indicated that it could be two conditions—a motor neuron disease (MND), which includes ALS, or a mild stroke.

On St. Patrick's Day, Steve and Mary were finally able to see a neurologist near Hudson, and he diagnosed it as ALS. Before this visit Steve never told Mary what he believed she might have. When the doctor said ALS, Mary was confused at first, but when she saw the look on Steve's face, she realized the severity of the diagnosis. They held hands during the silent ride home. There was so much unspeakable, unimaginable pain and fear in that doctor's office that day, and after the tears were emptied, dead shock. Breathe. Pray. And move forward.

The weekend after the neurologist's appointment Mary felt chest pain that resulted in a 911 call and a trip to the local ER. It turned out to be a panic attack, but this would be the first of many ER and hospital visits in the next 3+ years.

Life continued at The Outpost with Mary, Steve, and Mya. Mya had an abundance of energy, but because of the demands of managing Mary's disease while working and taking care of everything else, Mya was never trained. Mary loved Mya, and her name was one of the last words Mary was able to speak. She would laugh when Mya would jump onto her lap and lick her face, her "Mya Mya." Mary's disease slowly separated her from the things she loved. Before leaving on a trip to Hudson one day, Steve left Mary with Mya near the car and ran into the bank to get some cash. He was only gone for a minute but when he returned to the car, he found her on the ground crying while holding onto Mya's leash. She was crushed because she no longer had the strength to walk her beloved Mya.

That April, a series of tests were done at the Cleveland Clinic to confirm the ALS diagnosis, and Mary began the weekly treatments and medications to slow down the progression. During this time Steve and our brother, Pete, teamed up to search for new treatments and trials. This resulted in Mary being accepted to one of the top ALS research/treatment centers in the U.S. in Boston. Mary and Steve made three trips to Boston looking for potential trials in which she could participate but had no success. During this time, they found out that Mary had a special gene sequence that was determined to be a good indicator that her ALS may be primarily genetic, which is considered to be the main driver for 10% of those who suffer from the disease.

Mary was a fighter. Her faith never wavered; it grew stronger. In August, she and Steve flew to San Diego to be there for Paige at the birth of her second grandson, Oliver. Steve made sure that Mary was wheeled into the delivery room for the birth. Mary loved her grandsons Owen and Oliver! In September, Steve and Mary drove to Boston to attend the Ride for ALS. Steve, Pete, and Christopher all finished the 50-mile ride to raise money for the ALS Foundation. Mary is the rock, the center of our faith, rejoicing in love.

Family pic from ALS with Mary in the center. Left to right: front row-Pete taking the selfie, his middle daughter, Alandra; middle row-Pete's wife, Kim, growing out of his head, Mary centered and Steve on the right; back row-Sally (Chris's then fiancé, now wife), Tebben with the hat, Chris growing out of Tebb's hat, Paula and me

In October 2016, our niece, Meredith Chandler Lopez (Merlo), married her fiancé, Chris Ruzzi, in San Diego. This was another huge event for our family. Tebben had only been home from Peru for a couple of months. She was one of Merlo's bridesmaids. Steve and Mary also made the trip. God's hand of grace is all over us.

In January 2017, Mary had a feeding tube put in. This required Steve to be home a lot for her feeding. He held it together. His faith was being challenged, but he was strong. He was determined to fight alongside Mary so she had everything she needed and received the best care possible. Steve was strong, but I knew he needed help. I felt a calling in my heart to be there for Mary, and Steve, but also for myself. I had crawled out of the dark pit, but at times I still felt like I was just holding on. That same month I drove to Cleveland to stay with Mary and Steve and work with Mary on her physical therapy and feeding tube. Steve hadn't been to his office since the feeding tube was put in.

I was there for two weeks, and this is when Mary and I really connected, heart to heart, prayer to prayer. We fueled each other's faith. She had been getting around fairly well with her walker, and the house had been modified for her care. There was a ramp from the driveway to the front door and an electric lift to take her upstairs to their bedroom. She was fighting and working hard into her healing. She was able get to the lift and go upstairs to lay down or use the bathroom. We got into a routine. Breakfast, Bible reading, prayer, PT, rest, lunch, Bible, PT, rest, then Steve comes home. We listened to worship music much of the day but also watched a lot of TV. Mary loved ABC, *Good Morning America,* the cooking shows in the afternoon and *The Bachelorette* at night. I'm tough with her on the PT, but she fought through it. She was living God's Word, "Therefore, strengthen your feeble arms and weak knees. 'Make level paths for your feet,' so that the lame will no longer be disabled but rather healed." Hebrews 12:12, 13

Steve and Mary decided to move to Dad's house in Commack so they could be closer to Boston, where there was a chance that she could participate in a study and be closer to family. Teresa lives 15 minutes away, and I'm an hour-and-a-half drive from Connecticut depending on the traffic. And Dad was still with us then and fully supportive to help them in any way he could. Pete and I went to Cleveland to help them drive to Long Island. We drove the rental truck, and Steve, Mary, and Mya drove in their Mazda.

I handled the truck for most of the eight-hour drive, and Pete white-knuckled it through my superior driving skills, which include driving an average of 80 MPH.

Steve and Mary lived in Commack from April 2017 until April 2018. Mary's condition continued to deteriorate, and she was cared for during the day by either a certified nurse's assistant or a licensed practical nurse. Steve's supervisor at GE was very sensitive and supportive throughout Steve and Mary's trial. Steve worked remotely but had to meet with his team in Cleveland for a week each month. I was blessed to be able to be in Commack during those times to take over Mary's care during the evenings and early mornings before her nurse would arrive. God had prepared me for this, starting with our Mom's gifts of healing and compassion as an ER nurse. She modeled this devotion for us, and we had seen her care for her parents, her mother-in-law; she even cared for Paula's father, Bill Gill, during the last few weeks of his life before he died at home.

My time spent with my friend Rich Macharolli, who also had ALS, brought me close to Rich and this disease. And Mary and I were both fired up for the Lord. When you have to help someone who is helpless with all of their physical needs, you really grow close to that person. You have to trust each other. We maintained our daily devotions.

After getting her up from bed to the bathroom, then into her chair, we would play contemporary Christian worship music and praise the Lord. Sometimes we would hear *That's What Faith Can Do,* which would make us sad. But when we heard another of our favorite songs, *I Can Only Imagine,* by Mercy Me, we would rejoice, and I would sing the lyrics which filled our hearts with joy: "*I can only imagine what it will be like when I walk by your side. I can only imagine what my eyes will see when your face is before me.*"

We continued to read the Bible and pray every day. Sometimes we prayed in the Spirit. As Mary's disease destroyed her body, her courage and faith grew stronger. She was amazing. She inspired me. She loved Jesus. She loved my brother. She loved her children, and her grandchildren. She loved us all. She loved life. Hundreds of people were following Mary on social media. She blessed them all. Her life helped me put things into perspective. She suffered so . . . slowly becoming helpless, unable to move, to communicate. Her faith was amazing to see, and God used it to make me stronger, a better man, heading in the direction he wanted me to go.

There were times when Mary cried out in anguish and pain. But she would always return to the rock of her faith. She believed.

When Steve and Mary returned to Ohio that April, Mary was placed in a facility in Bucyrus. She was there for two weeks until her breathing challenges led her to decide to have a tracheotomy on her birthday, May 9. Steve and Mary were in this together, but Mary was still in control of her life and making decisions about her health care. She was still living with her faith that God would heal her. Both Steve and I had conversations with her about whether she wanted to change her status to DNR (do not resuscitate) or remain on Full Code, which called for all efforts to be made to sustain her life. She chose to fight for each breath until the end. She wanted to hold on to what's most precious, life, love. And to suffer like Christ brought her closer to Him, until they were face to face; and being close to Mary, you were closer to God.

After Bucyrus, Mary was moved into a nursing facility in Greens Springs, Ohio, near her hometown of Fremont. Steve commuted daily from his apartment in Bucyrus, and Mary's hometown friends, Vickie and Becky, were there to provide support when they could.

The drive to Green Springs took 45 minutes, and Steve couldn't spend much time with Mya, which started taking a toll on her. Eventually, he found a foster home for Mya but didn't tell Mary right away. When he eventually told her, she cried but understood. Steve showed her pictures of Mya's new home and foster parents and how well she was being cared for. This helped, but Steve still felt like he had failed Mary in a way by not being able to keep her dog.

In November 2018 Mary was moved into St. Augustine Manor on the west side of Cleveland. Steve rented a two-bedroom apartment in Little Italy, that we called "The Slant" because the foundation was leaning and an office chair on wheels would roll across the floor. Nick moved into the apartment, which was only a couple of blocks from St. Augustine, to be close to his chef job about a mile away.

Steve spent most of his time by Mary's side. He got to know all the nurses, doctors, PAs, CNAs, maintenance guys at the hospital, and they got to know Steve. This wasn't always pleasant for the staff as Steve was determined to ensure that Mary received the best care possible. He had a lot of questions and was occasionally demanding. There was tough love happening at St. Augustine.

In the summer of 2019 Mary started to decline and became more and more unresponsive. Steve and the staff thought her time to leave this world would be dawning soon. Toward the end of July, I drove out to Cleveland to be with Steve and Mary. I stayed at The Slant and walked to St. Augustine to spend days with Mary. I don't exactly know what happened, but she made a brief comeback. We prayed, read the Bible and watched TV like we always did. I was working on my first book, *Hard Knocks: Memoir of a Small Moment,* and Mary agreed to allow me to read it to her. Perhaps the reading is what gave her that last burst of life because of how, at one point, she made it clear to me that she had heard enough!

Steve prepared to say goodbye to the love of his life, his true soul mate. It was through his relationship with her that he came to know Christ and grow in faith. Their journey together was the easiest and hardest thing he'd ever done. It was God's plan that they be together because Steve was the only man who could love her through her trial and stay by her side until the end.

Teresa and I drove out to Cleveland to be with Steve and Mary on August 13. He was barely holding up. The decision to take her off life support was all his. He just needed to have us there to hold him up should he fall. We gathered in Mary's room the morning of August 15. Her room was filled with her PA and nurses. Steve was by her side holding her hand for the last time. We were all there with him standing around her bed. Steve let her go, and her life support was removed. I have never been with someone at their moment of death.

Mary was calm, serene, at peace. There was no struggle, no labored breathing, no visible pain or suffering. She wasn't quite ready to go and stayed with us for about 20 minutes, breathing in the Holy Spirit, the breath of God, and releasing his love into that room. I felt the Lord's presence. It's hard to describe. Many have tried. I felt like I was in a place somewhere between the force of gravity and the spiritual realm where there is only light. I asked, and Steve gave his consent for me to speak to Mary and sing to her. I leaned next to her and spoke softly into her ear. I don't remember what I said, but I reached a point where I could no longer speak, could barely stand, and could only sing. I sang one of our favorite songs to Mary . . . *"I can only imagine when that day comes when I find myself standing in the sun/I could only imagine when all I will do is forever, forever worship you."*

and at 9:53 am,

Mary released her final breath and went to be with the Lord.

A sketch by Teresa of Mary and Steve embracing

"I have fought the good fight, I have finished the race, I have kept the faith. Now there is in store for me the crown of righteousness, which the Lord, the righteous judge, will award me on that day—and not only to me, but also to all who have longed for his appearing."

2 Timothy 4:7, 8

The memorial service for Mary was held on August 25. The funeral home was just up the block from the hospital. Many of the staff who cared for Mary during the year she spent at St. Augustine's were planning to attend. Her room was still empty. It was just before 10:00 am, when Ken, the respiratory technician, approached the nurse's station, passing by Mary's room, which was across the hall and visible from the station. He was checking his patients' notes when he was joined by Gwen, Steve's favorite nurse. They were talking about Mary when they saw the call light from her room switch on. Ken had a clear view of her room from the station and was certain that no one had entered. He was unnerved and asked Gwen to check it out. She entered the room, turned the light off and checked to see if the switch was working properly. It worked perfectly. Mary had just been sharing heaven's light.

"Aren't all angels ministering spirits sent to serve those who will inherit salvation." Hebrews 1:18

Mary was buried in Freemont, Ohio, on September 7, 2019. Steve offered the eulogy.

"Words are extremely hard for me to assemble right now when thinking of Mary, but once again I'll do my best and I'll keep this short.

I have been blessed with the gift of having her in my life these past 10+ years. From the moment I met this beautiful soul at a coffee shop in Stow, Ohio on our first date on October 15th, 2008, to her last breath on August 15th at St Augustine Manor, Mary has been my source of inspiration and the main driver behind my rebound in this world. Every day with her was like a holiday and what we shared together was beyond my wildest dreams, which is one of the reasons why I called her Mary Poppins in addition to her chosen profession as a nanny.

Mary navigated through a very challenging life with many obstacles and disappointments along with the way. But somehow she always dealt with it with a smile on her face and hope that what lie ahead in the future would be better. Faith was a cornerstone of her approach to life and with this in mind, I'd like to play the song Mary choose for our wedding . . . What Faith Can Do by Kutless . . . which

I believe she choose not only for our wedding but as a reminder to me to never give up and continue on.

Mary deeply loved her family and friends in an unconditional way, which is rare in the world these days. Although I never met her, I believe she learned this from her beloved mother, Glenna, as well as from the small, tight community she was raised in at Old Fort, Ohio. She now is at rest next her mother and is a few miles away from her childhood neighborhood so in essence she is back home.

Welcome home Mary and until we see each other again always remember that we love you! God bless you!"

Chapter 20

And So It Goes

DURING MY YOUTH, I went through The School of Hard Knocks. I barely got out alive. As prophesied by my father, I flew through the Cuckoo's Nest and landed in jail. I died to myself in Christ. During my young adulthood my heart was not hardened, and I found an impenetrable love, a Hard Love, that could not be broken. This Hard Love gave birth to Hard Faith, grown over the years, through all that is good and bad; it endures . . .

And So It Goes

And so it goes
we are born
and raised up
live our lives
love
hate
we are deceived
we are loved
adored
despised
we fight in the flesh
and the spirit
we rejoice
and weep

we pray
and doubt
we win
and lose
we are brave
and afraid
we dance
and sing
and we sleep
Deep Rem
and sweat through
sleepless nights
we feel birth
and death
we hear God's whisper
and the thunder of his voice
we are deaf to Glory
in pain
we ignore
we fly
and run
and walk
we are strong
and weak
we save
and destroy
we create
beauty
and destruction
but we choose faith
and hold on
in full embrace
or barely a touch
a breath
our lives
the blink of an eye
an endless vapor
but in the end
"The only thing that counts is faith expressing itself through
love." Galatians 5:6
And so it goes